All-Color Guide

Snakes

of the World by John Stidworthy

Illustrated by Dougal MacDougal

YDNEY

FOREWORD

Snakes are perhaps the most maligned and feared members of the entire animal kingdom. This is greatly to be regretted, not because they are all harmless — indeed, some are so dangerous that they should be avoided at all costs. But snakes have also been the victims of a great deal of popular lore that has obscured the fact that most snakes are harmless, often handsome and generally useful creatures. In this book, the popular conceptions — and misconceptions — are examined in perspective. With its superb illustrations and detailed descriptions, the book might well serve as a field guide as well as an armchair introduction to the realm of snakes.

SNAKES OF THE WORLD
*A Bantam Book / published by arrangement with
Grosset & Dunlap, Inc.*

PRINTING HISTORY
Grosset & Dunlap edition published January 1971

Bantam edition / February 1972
9th printings through April 1983

ISBN 0-553-23527-3

Published simultaneously in the United States and Canada

PRINTED IN _____ RICA

DP   18

CONTENTS

SNAKES: EVOLUTION AND DESCRIPTION

Snakes, together with lizards, alligators, crocodiles, turtles and the tuatara (a lizard-like species that has survived only in New Zealand), form the reptile class of the vertebrates, or backboned animals. Like the other vertebrates, reptiles—in addition to their backbones—have skulls, brains, sense organs, alimentary, excretory, and reproductive organs. It is not easy to single out a characteristic that distinguishes reptiles from all other vertebrates, but the former nearly always possess certain features. Basically land animals, reptiles breathe air into their lungs. With a few exceptions, which we shall examine shortly, reptiles lay eggs suitable for development on dry land, with hard or leathery shells and plenty of yolk to nourish the growing young. Reptiles have scaly skins,

Eastern Collared Lizard

and they are 'cold-blooded' like amphibians and fishes—that is, their body temperature depends on that of their surroundings.

Because the lizards are the closest relations of the snakes and have so many characteristics in common, lizards and snakes are usually classified together in the order (or superorder) Squamata (from the Latin for 'scaly'). In relation to other reptiles, the Squamata are not an ancient group, having been in existence for only about 160 million years, whereas the first reptiles appeared at least 100 million years previously. The snakes themselves are an even more recent group,

A cylindrical skink (top) and a slowworm (below)
are two of the many lizards that have evolved
to appear like snakes.

not appearing until Cretaceous times—about 125 million
years ago—and not beccomming common until the small
mammals that are their main food-source had also become
widespread. As might be expected, the Cretaceous snake
fossils had skeletons very different from modern snakes.

The snakes are believed to have evolved from lizard ancestors. How this came about has long been a point of argu-
ment, but it is thought that the lizards that were ancestral to
snakes took to a life of burrowing underground. In these cir-
cumstances, legs were of little use and were lost, and when
the animals returned to surface life millions of years later,
they were limbless. Many of the snake's other adaptations—for

Snakes appeared in the Cretaceous Period, and their ancient
fossils can sometimes be found.

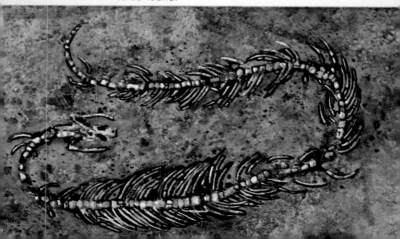

example, its shape and the type of eyes—also point to a burrowing origin.

When considering the various families of lizards, we find many species that are superficially snakelike; this is nearly always associated with burrowing habits. Most lizards that move on the surface have long legs, but those that move over soft soil or sand may have short legs and slither, like some skinks, with a tendency to be elongate. It is possible to find all grades of lizards, from those with well-developed limbs to those without any, including some with only one pair of limbs. The trend reaches a peak in the legless lizards, such as the slowworm, certain skinks, and several others including those commonly known as 'glass snakes.'

In spite of the fact that snakes evolved from lizards, and there are some lizards with one or two snakelike character-istics and vice versa, it is a fairly easy task to distinguish most modern snakes from lizards.

In snakes, with a few exceptions, there are no limbs or hip girdle and the shoulder girdles are always absent; in most lizards, limbs and girdles are present. The snake's skull forms a box around the front of the brain to prevent damage when feeding, while lizards have an open-fronted braincase. Snakes have very flexible jaws for dealing with their prey, whereas lizards have rigid jaws.

Apart from lack of legs, the obvious differences externally between snakes and lizards are in the sense organs and scales. Snakes invariably lack eyelids, but these are replaced by a transparent round spectacle, a cap or shield that covers the exposed portion of the eye. This is a modified version of the

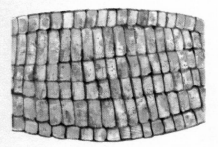

The belly scales of the lizard show no change in structure and the pattern continues along the body without a break.

Comparison of a snake head (*above*) with that of a lizard (*below*). The eyelid of the lizard is quite clearly seen to be absent in the snake. Note, too, the lizard's external ear.

body scales and is sloughed off with the skin at every molt. A few burrowing lizards have this kind of spectacle, and its origin can be imagined as a device that evolved for keeping out particles of dirt from the eyes during burrowing. Most lizards have a visible eardrum, but snakes never possess an external ear. The snake's scale pattern runs from the head down the body without a break. In lizards, there are always several rows of scales along the length of the belly; most snakes, with their specialized means of locomotion, have just a single row of scales on the ventral, or belly, surface. Thus, by looking at the combination of such features as eyes, ears and ventral scales, you should be able to tell snakes from lizards fairly readily.

There are also other differences. Typical snakes have only one lung, whereas lizards have two, and there are many small differences in the design of the skeleton and viscera. These, however, cannot be seen in the living animal.

Snakes have a single row of scales on their ventral surface adapted to their special means of locomotion.

Physical Background

A snake has internal organs very similar to those of other reptiles—indeed, to other vertebrates. The problem is that the snake has to contain these organs in an exceedingly long and narrow body cavity; a rather unusual arrangement evolved to cope with this.

In one respect, the shape of the snake is ideal. There is no necessity for having a long coiled gut in a short wide abdomen—the condition in most vertebrates. Long intestines are necessary to provide a large surface area for the digestion and absorption of food. In a snake, the alimentary canal passes straight down the body from mouth to vent with no coiling, except in the region of the small intestine. The stomach is simply a somewhat enlarged portion of the gut and does not lie across the body cavity as it does in most vertebrates.

Although the shape of the snake's body makes the arrangement of the gut simple and efficient, it is more difficult to accommodate those organs, such as lungs and kidneys, that vertebrates usually possess in pairs, one on each side of the body. The snake's answer to this problem is, either to arrange members of the pair one behind the other, or to eliminate one of the pair completely. The kidneys are arranged behind one another, right in front of left, and so are the testes or ovaries. The organ on the right side is generally larger than the left, and both are very elongated. The liver is also elongated with a smaller left lobe and a highly developed right lobe. The gall bladder has been squeezed out from its usual location next to the liver to a position just below it. The urinary bladder has been eliminated entirely.

The same form of development can be seen in the lungs. Most snakes have only one functional lung, the right; even those snakes with two lungs have the left one poorly developed. The lung usually extends more than half the length of the body. The hind part seems to function just as an air reservoir, while the front part and a specially developed windpipe are concerned with taking in oxygen. Instead of having complete rings of cartilage around the windpipe like most vertebrates, snakes have incomplete cartilaginous rings and the membrane in the part of the windpipe close to the lung has a porous lining like the functional part of the lung.

The blood system of the snake does not differ greatly from

INTERNAL ORGANS OF A HOG-NOSED SNAKE

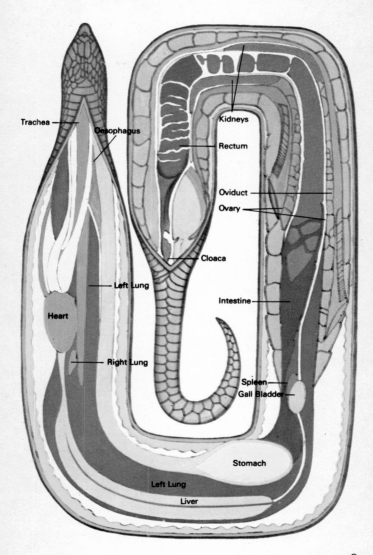

Trachea

Oesophagus

Kidneys

Rectum

Oviduct

Ovary

Left Lung

Cloaca

Heart

Intestine

Right Lung

Spleen

Gall Bladder

Stomach

Left Lung

Liver

Snake Skeleton

that of other reptiles. The heart is also similar to that of other reptiles—especially that of lizards—but extra blood vessels serve some of the elongated organs.

As well as possessing an unusual arrangement of the internal organs, the skeleton of the snake also has a number of interesting adaptations. The skull is, of course, specially modified for the feeding habits (see p. 29). The backbone also has some unusual features. Since there are no legs or limb girdles, none of the vertebrae needs to be specially modified for their attachment. Even in those snakes where a vestigial hip girdle is present, there is no connection between this and the backbone. Each vertebra in the backbone is similar to the next, all except the first one or two having ribs; in the tail region, ribs are fused to the vertebrae. The most remarkable feature of the backbone is the large number of vertebrae that it contains, the total varying from about 180 in the short-bodied vipers to as many as 400 or more in some of the pythons and the colubrids.

If we consider the flexibility needed to move in the manner of snakes, it can be seen that it is necessary to have either large numbers of vertebrae or else a large degree of flexibility between them. The large number gives a stronger vertebral column and involves less likelihood of damage to the spinal cord. The interlocking of one vertebra with another is rather complicated, with a ball-and-socket joint made by a round projection from the rear of one vertebra fitting into a hollow in the front of the next. As in other reptiles, there are also two bony prongs, or zygapophyses, stretching forward to touch similar projections from the back of the vertebra in front. Snakes also have an extra pair of projections on the back and front of each vertebra. Each vertebra, therefore, articulates with the next at five points, giving strong joints able to stand the stresses on them. Each joint is not in itself very flexible, bending only a few degrees in a vertical direction, although it will bend up to twenty-five degrees horizontally. The combination of large numbers of these joints gives the snake its flexibility.

Snake vertebrae viewed from the bottom (*top*) and the side (*below*).

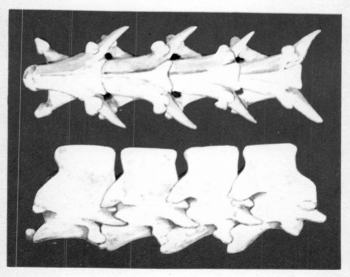

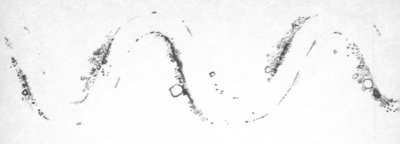

The undulating movement typical of most snakes can plainly be seen from the tracks the thrust leaves in the sand.

Snakes have several means of propulsion. In most cases, though, it is easier for the snake to move than it is for a human observer to explain how it does so.

The basic method of locomotion is by wriggling the body using complicated muscles ranged down either side of the backbone. The muscles are shortened on one side of the body, the contraction starting at the head and moving backward along the length of the snake. Following this, a wave of contraction is sent down the other side of the body from head to tail. As a snake is relatively long, not all the muscles on one side are contracted at the same time, with the effect that the body is thrown into horizontal waves, or undulations, as the muscles pull first to one side then the other. If a snake is placed on a perfectly smooth surface, such as glass, these movements fail to propel the snake anywhere since there must be something for it to push against.

On ordinary ground, small irregularities in the surface provide the necessary points of resistance. As the body-waves

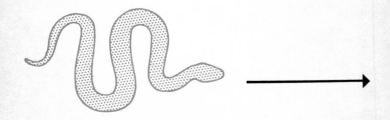

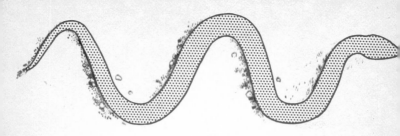

move down the snake, the outer and rear parts of each body-loop come into contact with the irregularities.

This resistance is sufficient to stop the loop moving backward on the ground and, as the snake is exerting muscular effort at this point, it propels part of the body forward. The result is usually that, while the snake sends waves of contraction along its body and moves steadily forward, the position of each loop relative to the ground remains stationary, the tail moving steadily along the track left by the head end. Long thin snakes are more efficient at moving in this way because they can have more body-loops, and therefore more points for pushing on the ground. If a snake moves through sand, a higher pile of sand is thrown up in the rear and outer parts of each loop, indicating the thrust.

This undulating movement is the one used by the majority of snakes, but there are others that involve looping the body. Some snakes can move through wide channels or burrows by a kind of concertina movement, throwing out loops at the front of the body to press against the walls of the track and to grip while they draw up the rear part of the body. The rear is then looped and pressed against the walls while the head end is straightened and moved forward.

The concertina form of movement employed by some snakes involves moving only one half of the body at a time.

In the shifting sand of deserts live vipers and rattle-snakes that employ a very special means of locomotion known as sidewinding. On loose sand it is impossible to get a proper grip with the sideways undulations that most snakes use, so side-winding snakes move along by pushing downward rather than horizontally. A snake that is sidewinding throws a loop of the front end of the body forward and places its neck on the ground. The rest of the body is then twisted forward clear of the ground, to lie in front of the head and neck in the direction the snake is moving. The fore parts touch the ground first, followed by the rest of the snake and eventually the tail. However, long before the tail reaches the ground, the snake has thrown its head and neck to a new position forward and sideways, and the rest of the body follows. The result of this is that usually only two short lengths of the snake's body touch the ground at one time, and it appears to be spiraling along sideways,

A sidewinding snake *(left)* leaves a series of tracks shaped like a capital J.

14

leaving a series of tracks shaped like a capital J. The crook is where the neck was placed with the head facing forward, and the stem of the J is formed by the body as it is brought forward in front of the neck. Lastly, the crosspiece is made by the tail as it pushes clear of the ground.

Quite different from any of the other snake methods of moving is rectilinear creeping. This is usually only seen in those snakes with very thick bodies—such as pythons and vipers—but for some of them it is the preferred method of getting about. Keeping the body in an almost straight line, the snake pulls forward a belly scale, slightly lifting it by using muscles attached to the ribs. Another muscle pulls the scale backward and the free hind edge catches on the ground, propelling the snake forward. Belly scales are moved in this way one after the other, and the snake creeps slowly forward. The snake does not move its ribs when creeping in this manner, but uses them as stationary points from which the muscles moving the scales can work; the skin must be loose and able to move freely over the body musculature. This form of locomotion is of little use to a snake needing to go fast, and even pythons use the normal undulatory movements at those times.

Generally, most snakes are able to employ whatever means of progression suits them in a certain situation. They may commonly use one sort of locomotion, but if the need arises can use another; for instance, even the Old World watersnake may sidewind on soft sand, although rather inefficiently.

Rectilinear creeping of heavy snakes uses movement of belly scales.

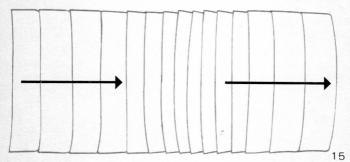

The skin of snakes has evolved to meet some very exacting requirements. It must be smooth, providing very little frictional resistance to forward movement so as not to impede the snake; at the same time, it must be rough enough to be able to grip and push on obstacles when pushed backward. The skin must also be very flexible, but still tough enough not to wear away as the snake moves along. These requirements are met in snakes by a skin of overlapping scales with their free edges pointing to the rear. They are tough enough not to wear out quickly and smooth enough not to provide resistance to moving forward, although snake scales are neither wet nor slimy. The free edges of the scales point backward and provide a grip for locomotion; in particular, the large belly scales are specially adapted to this job.

The scales of snakes are not separate pieces of skin, but are formed of folded skin. Thick portions of the outer layers, the epidermis, form the scales. This continues between the scales but is thinner and folded into pleats. Between the belly scales, the folds are simple; on the back, where the scales are not arranged in a simple straight line, the folds must necessarily be more complicated. This arrangement of scales and folds of skin gives flexibility to the snake's covering and also allows quite a degree of distension, a necessary feature to swallow bulky prey.

Like the skin of other vertebrates, the skin of a snake is composed basically of three layers. The thick innermost layer is soft, fibrous, and pliable. This inner layer, the dermis, contains the pigment cells and provides the snake with its characteristic colors and patterns. Outside this is a layer of cells, the epidermis, which produces the third layer, an external covering made of a horny substance called keratin. The same substance forms hair and nails in mammals, and the keratin of a snake is exceptionally tough. On the outside of a snake's scales, the layer of keratin is only about two-thousandths of an inch thick, but this is enough to resist normal wear and tear and to protect the snake from injury. Keratin has virtually no stretching qualities, however, but the highly folded skin between scales makes up for this.

Other ways that snakes are able to move are by the processes of swimming, climbing, and flying. Of all these types of locomotion, swimming appears to be the most natural ability—presumably because of the similarity between the ordinary motions of swimming and crawling.

In the same way that snakes are able to swim, most also possess the ability to climb. The concept of a snake winding around a tree or pole is incorrect; to ascend something that is not too smooth, the snake uses a modified concertina action. The snakes that climb well are found to have special belly scales forming an angle on each side of the body; these corners catch on tree bark and give good support to the body. A few species have slender bodies that can be supported by light vegetation and are able to crawl through any plants strong enough to support them.

Some Asiatic species of snakes are often said to fly, although this term is not being used precisely in such cases. Most of the species are those that already live in the trees and have the ability to leap from tree to tree. They hold their bodies parallel to the ground so that resistance to the air breaks the speed of their fall. The snakes that do this have slender bodies that they can flatten or even make concave along the ventral side.

Snakes are frequently thought of as fast-moving animals, but this is, in fact, an illusion combined with ignorance of reptilian metabolism. A snake can move fast only for a very short distance before it has to slow down due to the slow rate of oxygenation of its blood. Normally a snake crawls at truly a snail's pace.

Even the outer layer of the skin of a snake eventually wears out, but it is replaced in quite a different way from the thin horny covering of the human skin. Humans continually produce keratin over the epidermis from the inside at the same time as this keratin is worn away at the outside. The change in snakes is much more abrupt: the snake periodically grows a complete new covering. A new epidermis is grown beneath the old, and not until it is fully formed does the snake lose the old outer skin. This process is known as molting.

When a snake has grown a new epidermis and is about to shed its skin, it secretes a thin layer of fluid between the old and new skin (which are no longer touching) giving the snake a clouded milky appearance. This can be seen especially

17

at the eyes, for the milky fluid covers the pupils and makes the snake almost, if not completely, blind. This condition may last for as much as a week; during this period, snakes normally remain in hiding.

A day or two after the cloudiness has cleared, the snake will shed its skin. This is accomplished by opening and stretching the mouth and rubbing it on surrounding objects until the old skin at the edges of the lips begins to split. Rubbing continually, the snake starts to wriggle out of its skin. This is usually sloughed off in one piece from head to tail, turned inside-out in the process by the emerging snake. Sometimes

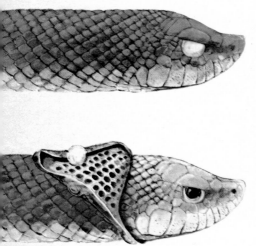

Before the snake sheds its skin it has a milky appearance and fluid covers the eye (*top*). The skin begins to split at the edge of the lips and the snake will start to wriggle out of it (*bottom*).

the skin will break up, however, and come off in pieces, as during the shedding of lizards.

The sloughed-off skin is a perfect cast of the snake. The large belly scales, the pattern of scales on the back, the eye spectacle and even casts of facial pits can all be seen. It is completely devoid of color as the pigment cells remain in the dermis, which is never shed. The shed skin is transparent with a white tinge. After it has been detached from the snake for a while, it usually becomes brittle. The sloughed-off skin is not especially attractive, but the newly

18

emerged snake is seen at its best. Most species show their best bright colors in the days immediately following molting; as the upper skin gets older, the colors do not show through as well.

The skin is not shed at regular intervals, nor does molting seem dependent on the snake's growth. A whole variety of factors—health, the temperature of the environment, emergence from hibernation, amount of food taken—all seem to have their effect. Most snakes molt three or four times a year, but for young specimens and some particular species, the rate may be higher. Alternatively, though, some species apparently shed only once a year.

The snake wriggles out of its old skin, which turns inside-out (*left*) and usually sloughs off the skin in one piece (*right*).

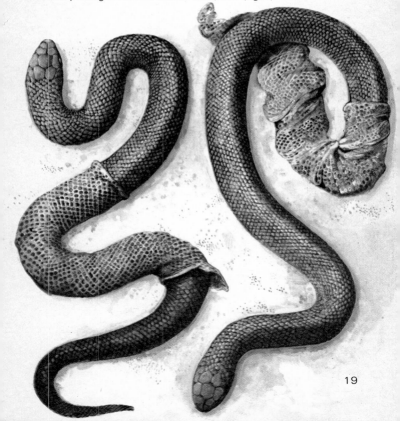

The Senses

Snakes possess the human senses, as well as many others, but their sense organs are unusual in their structure and function somewhat differently.

Snakes' eyes, for example, differ even from those of their closest relatives, the lizards, probably because the burrowing ancestors of snakes had useless, degenerate eyes. Snakes redeveloped reasonably good eyes from the rudiments that

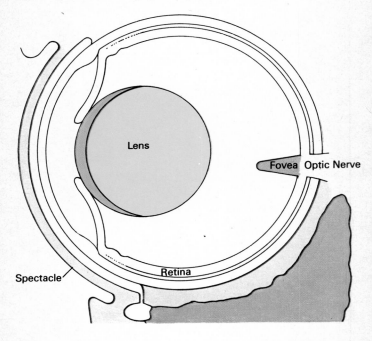

A typical snake eye, with an untypical fovea.

were left, but having lost some of the parts of the lizard eye, had to do things in a different way. The snake has a spectacle instead of eyelids. And instead of changing the focus of the eye by using muscles to change the shape of the lens, as lizards or men do, the snake changes focus by moving the lens forward. The snake lens is round and can not easily change shape. The lens is also yellow and seems to work as a color filter, a function performed by yellow oil-drops in the retina of lizards. The light-sensitive cells of the retina include both rods, which are sensitive to small amounts of light, and cones, which give sharpness of vision and are often associated with color vision. Snakes have double cones, structures that are never found in lizards and are yet another indication of the independent evolution of the eye by snakes. Although the snake possesses cones, it has yet to be proved that they have the true color vision of the lizards.

The snake eye is very short-sighted. To obtain sharp images, a special region of the retina, the fovea, is used, where many cones are closely packed together. A small number of tree snakes have a fovea, but most snakes are without one and presumably unable to see things as sharply as humans. It is also doubtful whether snakes with eyes on the side of the head can judge distances well, although a few tree snakes may be able to by looking forward with both eyes down grooves in their

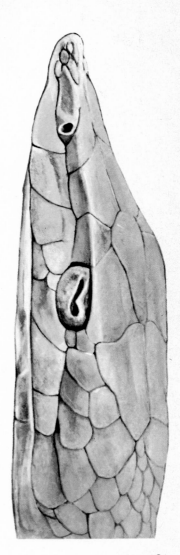

The tree snake is one of the few snakes able to see things sharply.

snout. In general, the snake's eyes seem to function as movement-detectors over a wide field, rather than providing detailed images. Immobile prey may not be recognized.

In snakes the eardrum and middle ear—which in lizards receive air-borne sounds—have disappeared. This again is probably a result of the snake's burrowing ancestry, when airborne sounds were of no significance. The bone that conducts sounds from the eardrum to the inner ear in the lizard is, in a snake, attached to the inside of the jaw bones. As a consequence, the snake is completely deaf to sounds in the air, although any vibration on the ground, such as that caused by a footfall, may be transmitted to the inner ear via the bones of the skull. In this way, the snake 'hears' vibrations.

The inner ear of a snake, like that of a man, is involved with maintaining balance. The nose is quite large, and seems to possess a good sense of smell, but even more important to a snake for recording chemical stimuli is a sense organ known as Jacobson's organ. This is a pair of cavities in the roof of the mouth that have a lining similar to that of the sensory part of the nose. Jacobson's organ is used in conjunction with the tongue, which is long and forked in a snake; the tongue is not a sting and is possessed by harmless and venomous snakes. The tongue flickers in and out of the mouth, picking up small particles from the air or ground and taking them inside the mouth; there the forked tip of the tongue is placed in Jacobson's organ. This then 'tastes-smells' what the tongue has picked up. For a snake, and

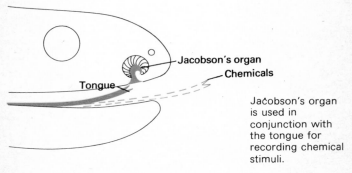

Jacobson's organ is used in conjunction with the tongue for recording chemical stimuli.

The tongue of the snake collects small particles that its Jacobson's organ then tastes-smells.

also for some lizards, this accessory sense of 'taste-smell' seems more important than the real nose. Jacobson's organ enables snakes to trail prey or potential mates and aids identification of objects in the surroundings. The tongue itself has no sense of taste, but it is constantly in motion in an exploring or disturbed snake.

As well as the specialized sense organs of the head, snakes, like man, possess sensory endings distributed over the whole skin. The whole skin of a snake, in spite of its scaly nature, is sensitive to touch; there may be specialized touch-receptors as well, such as the small organs found around the chin and vent of many colubrid snakes that are used in courtship. Receptors sensitive to warmth are also distributed generally over the body; a few snakes, such as rattlesnakes, have developed specialized heat receptors as well (see p. 130).

Snakes are well equipped, therefore, to explore their immediate surroundings by the different senses of taste-smell and touch and through the ability to sense vibrations. The eyes and other sense organs of the snake, however, are incapable of helping to tell what is happening any great distance away.

Enemies

Snakes have many enemies. Perhaps the worst is man, who destroys their habitat and through fear or ignorance kills individuals, but many other foes take their toll. There are many species of snake that are snake-eaters—some, like the king cobra and king snakes, specialize in this diet, others only occasionally. The shape of the snake makes it an easy object to swallow, and snakes may eat others almost as large as themselves. Other reptiles may also feed on snakes if given the chance; a few snakes, usually young ones, even suffer the ignominy of being swallowed by frogs. Many species of birds, including ground hornbills and many hawks, will attack snakes. Farmers in Africa sometimes keep tame secretary birds because snakes are a favorite part of their diet.

Most smaller carnivorous mammals eat snakes; but although many have been found with snakes in their stomachs, none seems to have a main diet of snakes. Even the mongoose, often imagined as archenemy of snakes, only attacks them at chance encounters. The pig is a far more persistent snake-hunter and will trample a snake to death before eating it.

Most of the mammals and birds that attack snakes are not

In combat with a cobra, a mongoose
erects its stiff hair and relies on its ability to
dodge a strike.

Snakes are a favorite part of the diet of a secretary bird.

immune to poisonous venom but rely on their speed and agility. Some do, however, have partial immunity. Mongooses, for instance, are considered to be more resistant to cobra venom than are most mammals of their size. Even so, a well-directed snake-bite can be fatal. The mongoose may attack by darting in to bite the back of the snake's neck or may seize the snake by its jaws, so it can no longer use its fangs, and simply hold on until the snake has exhausted itself with struggling. The snake does not have the reserves of energy of a mongoose and will tire first. In fact, unless the snake makes a lucky strike, mongoose versus cobra is a one-sided contest.

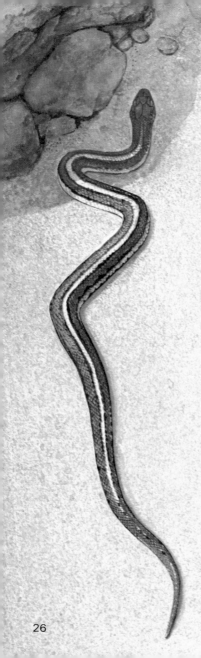

Snakes are said to be cold-blooded. This does not mean they are cold but that they do not control their temperature and keep it at a constant level as do mammals and birds—by their internal metabolism. A snake's temperature is dependent on that of its surroundings; in a warm place a snake is warm, while in a cold place it has a low temperature. This characteristic has important consequences in a reptile's life, for animal bodies function well only when they are warm and the snake is no exception to this. For this reason, most snakes are found in the warmer regions, and the number of species falls sharply with distance from the tropics. Few snakes live in cool temperate regions, none near the poles.

In spite of the fact that snakes are unable to generate much heat within their body tissues, they do manage to control their temperature to a certain extent by moving from one place to another. Snakes are fond of warming themselves, especially in the cooler parts of their ranges, by

Snakes can keep their temperature more or less constant for quite long periods by controlling the amount of body exposed to the sunlight.

basking in the sun. Basking in the sun, combined with exercise, may give a snake a slightly higher temperature than its surroundings. On the other hand, a snake that is becoming too hot will move to shelter in the shade. A snake will die if it becomes too hot (more than about 104° F.) or if its tissues freeze; by moving to the right places, it can usually avoid this fate.

The size and color of a snake will influence how quickly it warms up. Dark colors absorb heat faster than light ones, and, as a general rule, snakes from cold places have darker hues. This enables them to reach, or maintain, the optimum temperature more easily than might otherwise be the case. The reason that the really big snakes are tropical is probably that, if they lived in temperate climates, their huge bodies would take so long to warm up each day that there would be no time left for vital activities such as hunting.

Snakes in temperate regions have to undergo a period of enforced rest; they hibernate every winter. A snake left exposed to winter cold would surely die; if not frozen immediately, its body would be so chilled that escape from predators would be impossible. To avoid this, snakes seek a retreat at the onset of winter, below ground or in a hollow tree, where they will not be exposed to frost. Often many individual snakes will go to the same retreat, or hibernaculum, and it is not rare to find snakes hibernating with other snakes that are usually their prey.

In winter, many snakes retreat into a hibernaculum.

Feeding

All snakes are purely carnivorous and always eat what they kill whole. It might be supposed that, with their long thin bodies and heads, snakes would feed on small animals. In fact, relative to their size, snakes eat the biggest meals of all land vertebrates. Naturally this needs special adaptation and the skin and skull must be distensible. Instead of a solid upper jaw structure, the snake has developed a loosely bound system of bones held to one another and the rest of the skull by elastic ligaments. Each bone can move in relation to the other, and can be swung upward and outward. The lower jaw articulates with the quadrate bones, two long bones connected to the sides of the rear of the skull. The quadrate is movable and can swing downward and outward to open the jaw wide. The two halves of the bottom jaw also separate in the midline where they are joined only by an elastic ligament. Therefore, the mouth can be opened so wide that the jaws can be extended to deal with a meal two or three times the diameter of the resting snake's head.

The teeth are pointed, well designed for grabbing prey, but useless for chewing. They have no roots, are rather loosely attached to the jaw, and are replaced successively throughout life. They do, however, play an important part in keeping a grip on the prey during feeding. The sides of the jaw walk forward alternately, the right upper and lower jaw holding the prey while the left side is pushed forward. Then the teeth of the left take hold while the right is moved. The mouth is gradually eased around the prey until the muscles of the throat grip it and carry it down. While the snake has food blocking its mouth and throat, special muscles carry the windpipe forward so that it protrudes at the front of the jaw and the snake can still breathe.

Although the snake does not chew its food, digestion begins in the mouth with the production of saliva that also eases the swallowing process. The saliva of some harmless snakes is mildly toxic to their prey, so that venom can simply be seen as a kind of super saliva that kills and starts digestion before the food is swallowed.

An Old World watersnake devouring a frog, a common prey of many snakes.

Breeding and Development

Female snakes in breeding condition produce a special scent from their skin or sometimes from their anal glands. Males seek the female by following their scent-trails with flickering tongues. Before the female will allow the male to mate, a ritual courtship takes place. In most snakes, this consists of the male rubbing his chin along the back and flanks of the female toward the neck, flicking his tongue as he goes. This serves the dual purpose of stimulating the female—or at least lowering her inclination to move away—and stimulating the male on the special touch receptors on his chin. In most snakes the female plays a passive part, but in the Indian cobra and Aesculapian snake a courtship dance takes place. This may continue for many minutes before mating.

In mating, the penis of the male is inserted into the female and sperm is transferred. The penis of a snake is a double structure, only one half (the 'hemipene') being used at a time. It is often furnished with spines to lock it into the female so that

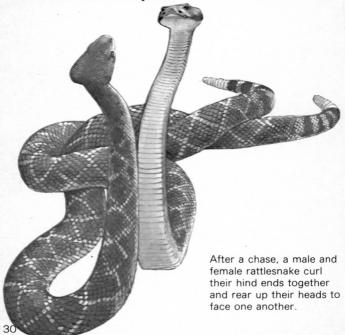

After a chase, a male and female rattlesnake curl their hind ends together and rear up their heads to face one another.

30

once mating is started it reaches a successful conclusion, even if the female begins to move around again.

A phenomenon that occurs in many species of snake during the mating season is the combat dance. Two male snakes meet, rear up, intertwine, and use the weight of their bodies to try to force the other off balance. There is no biting or angry hissing, but one snake eventually flees. Rivalry for females or territory have been put forward as reasons for this ritualized combat, but as yet nobody has given a satisfactory explanation for the function of this behavior.

Sperm may be stored in the female for some while after mating, and she may subsequently lay several clutches of fertile eggs from one mating, although mating and egg-laying more usually occur annually. In temperate regions, the mating season normally follows shortly after hibernation.

The eggs of snakes have parchment-like shells, and inside there is a large amount of yolk to provide food for the developing young. The mother snake usually seeks out a

Mating is accomplished when the male rattlesnake throws a body loop across the female and twines their tails together so their cloacas are opposite one another.

suitable nest, which may be a crevice in a wall, a burrow, under leaves, or even in manure. As well as giving protection, many of the chosen nest-sites have the advantage of being warm. Once the eggs are laid, in most cases the mother takes no further interest in them. The surroundings of the eggs must do the work of incubation. The yolk provides all the food the embryo needs to become a miniature replica of its parents and hatch. Once it has hatched, the newborn snake looks after itself.

A few snakes look after their young and construct a nest for their eggs. King cobras scoop piles of vegetation into a mound, in which they make two compartments. In the lower, the mother lays about three dozen eggs and then remains on top of them. The eggs are kept warm by the decaying vegetation and also by having the mother there. King cobras have been known to form monogamous pairs, both members protecting the nest. But, in general, snakes have no family ties and mate indiscriminately with others of their species.

Pythons do not construct nests, but some species remain coiled round the eggs after they are laid. Similar behavior has been seen in a few other kinds of snakes, and it has sometimes been said that they are incubating the eggs. Although the eggs are undoubtedly protected, it is not incubation in

A blue racer laying eggs.

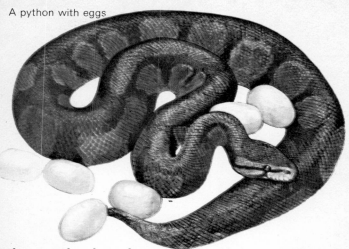

A python with eggs

the sense that the snakes are warming the eggs. At least one species of python has been reported as having a temperature slightly higher than that of the surrounding air while incubating, but it is not known how widespread this practice is nor how important it is for hatching the eggs.

Most egg-laying, or oviparous, snakes lay large clutches. This is necessary because of the many predators likely to eat the eggs, or later on, the young.

The time taken for snakes' eggs to hatch can vary considerably. Partly this depends on how soon they are laid. Some snakes lay eggs a few days after mating; some, like the European grass snake, do not lay until two months after mating. In the latter case, development of the embryo has already been pro-

King cobras make a mound as a nest for their eggs.

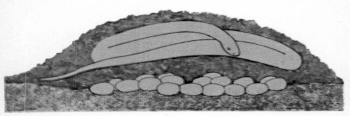

Most snakes are egg-laying, or oviparous, and the young snake is equipped with an egg-tooth with which it cuts itself out of its shell.

ceeding for some time, and the unborn snake spends a shorter period in the egg. The speed at which the eggs reach hatching-point also depends on the temperature, and they will develop faster in warm surroundings.

By the time the baby snake has grown large enough to hatch, it has developed an egg-tooth, a small pointed tooth at the tip of the upper jaw, that plays a vital part in its hatching. It is this egg-tooth that enables the young snake to cut itself out of the shell. After the strenuous effort of slashing the egg open, the little snake may rest for hours before emerging into the world. In most cases, the egg-tooth, having served its purpose, drops off after a few hours.

Most snakes are oviparous, which means they lay eggs, but some give birth to living young. This is not really so great a difference as it sounds. The snakes that give birth to live young are not comparable to mammals in their care of the young. All they do is retain their eggs inside their oviducts until a late stage of development, so that the eggs hatch as they are laid. In almost all cases, the embryo snakes have been obtaining nourishment from the yolk of their eggs just like any other embryo snake, and not from their mother. A very small number of snakes do have a primitive kind of placenta.

When born, the baby snake may remain in its embryonic membranes for a short while and must struggle free. This condition of retaining eggs and giving birth to young is known as ovoviviparity. It has obvious advantages for snakes that live in hostile climates because it gives the eggs a much better chance of hatching in a favorable environment. The mother, trying to reach optimum conditions of warmth, will carry the eggs with her, protecting them at the same time. Snakes that live in the coldest climates tend to be the ones that utilize this method, but others have also found it useful. In general, broods produced by ovoviviparous snakes are smaller than those of oviparous ones, presumably because there is a higher rate of survival of eggs, but even some live-bearing snakes have broods of over seventy young.

Growth in young snakes is usually rapid. In temperate regions where the young are hatched or born in late summer, there will probably be little time before hibernation; the

A few snakes give birth to living young.

snake will need to find enough food to last the winter. The next spring, growth will really begin. Year-old European vipers have been measured at one and one-half times their birth-length, but some snakes grow even faster. Rattlesnakes may double, and some pythons nearly treble, their length in the first year. Much depends on the species, climate, food available, and even the individual. In tropical snakes, growth may continue through the year; where hibernation is necessary, the snake grows fast in summer and not at all in winter. In successive years, growth continues but gradually slows down. In snakes and other reptiles, however, growth may never completely cease as it does in birds and mammals after they become sexually mature. A snake may go on growing through-out its life; but, whereas in the early years the increase in length may be very large, in an old snake it is scarcely mea-surable. Unlike mammals, mature reptiles still retain car-tilaginous ends to the bones, allowing the possibility of growth.

Snakes in warm climates mature sooner than those from cool climates; sexual maturity may be reached at from any-thing to one year in some snail-eating snakes, to five or six years in some snakes from temperate climates. About three or four years old is probably the average age of maturity.

It is very difficult to know exactly how long snakes live in the wild. No human has ever kept a wild snake under obser-vation all its life. From specimens taken in the wild and from experience in zoos it is estimated that some of the larger species might have a life expectancy of 20 or more years and that the smaller species may live from 10 to 15 years.

Below is a table of some snakes whose long lives in captivity have been authenticated.

Years in Captivity	Species
29	Black-necked Cobra
	Anaconda
27	Rainbow Boa
25	Indigo Snake
23	Boa Constrictor
	Leopard Snake
21	Corn Snake
	Cottonmouth

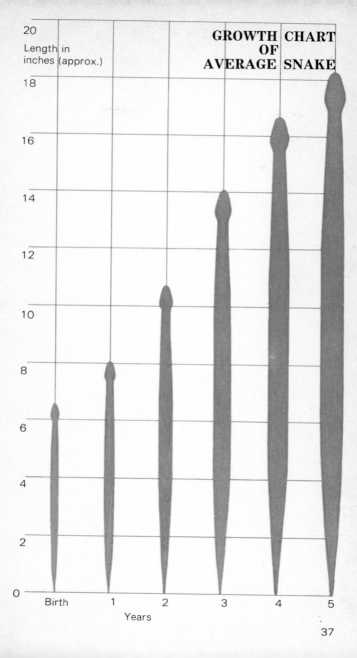

GROWTH CHART
OF
AVERAGE SNAKE

Length in inches (approx.)

Years

Birth 1 2 3 4 5

CLASSIFICATION OF SNAKES

It cannot be stated with certainty exactly how many species of snake live in the world today. Over 13,000 different kinds have been named; until more is known about many of them, it is impossible to be sure that they are all different species. As with other groups of animals, further knowledge may bring a reduction in the number of forms now believed to exist.

Like many other animals, snakes will not always fit neatly

TABLE OF THE SNAKE FAMILIES

SQUAMATA	SNAKES	with limb remnants	burrowers	all teeth in upper jaw
				all teeth in lower jaw
				eyes with spectacle
			surface dwellers	
	no limb remnants	two lungs		spiny shield on tail
		one lung		no poison fangs
				or back fanged
			rigid fangs	on land
				in sea
				folding fangs

LIZARDS

Venomous

into man-made categories, especially as different men may have different ideas on what the categories ought to be.

The following table divides the snakes into ten families, giving the approximate number of species belonging to each. Some zoologists would say that the seasnakes and cobras both belong in one family; some would separate the Viperidae into two different families—the vipers and pit vipers; some would separate the boas and pythons into two families. Until zoologists completely understand how snakes evolved, it is probable there will always be arguments on points such as these.

Family	Number of Species	Common name
Typhlopidae	200	BLIND SNAKES
Leptotyphlopidae	40	THREAD SNAKES
Anilidae	10	PIPE SNAKES
Boidae	100	BOAS AND PYTHONS
Uropeltidae	40	SHIELDTAILS
Xenopeltidae	1	SUNBEAM SNAKE
Colubridae	2500	TYPICAL SNAKES
Elapidae	150	COBRAS
Hydrophidae	50	SEASNAKES
Viperidae	80	VIPERS

The Smaller Families
Typhlopidae
The blind snakes are a family of primitive and specialized snakes found in most of the warm parts of the world. There are nearly 200 species. Nearly all blind snakes are small, about eight inches long, although one species grows to over two feet long. All are burrowers, and in external appearance are more like worms than snakes.

Blind Snake

These snakes are cylindrical in shape with a small head. The eyes are tiny with no spectacles, covered over with the same tiny, heavily overlapping scales that cover the rest of the body, including the ventral surface. The short tail often ends in a spine, presumably used in burrowing, and the scales are very smooth. The skull is rigid and the front of the head has a single plate for pushing through earth. Blind snakes are harmless, egg-laying insect-eaters, and the skin is sloughed off in rings.

Uropeltidae
Found only in India and Ceylon, the shieldtails are a family of only about 40 species. They are less than a foot long and are burrowers with small scales on both belly and back. The skull is rigid and the eyes are buried beneath scales.

The shieldtails get their name from the large shieldlike scale at the back of the tail, which is sometimes furnished with spines. The tail is used to take a firm grip on the soil as the snake straightens its body like a worm. The tail is then pulled forward by the strong muscles of the front of the body, and dug in again for another push. Shieldtails feed on

worms and other small soft creatures and are often bright colors. They lay no eggs but give birth to about six young at a time.

Leptotyphlopidae

The thread snakes, or slender blind snakes, are a small family of about 40 species living mainly in semi-arid regions of Africa, southwest Asia and the New World.

They are similar in external appearance to the blind snakes but are even smaller and thinner; they differ in that all the teeth are in the lower jaw, whereas those of the blind snakes are all in the upper jaw. The thread snakes also have vestiges of hind limbs in the shape of claws and a fairly complete pelvis; the blind snakes have no pelvis or only a small piece of bone as a remnant.

Thread snakes' food consists largely of termites. Like the blind snakes, the thread snakes are burrowers, rarely emerging on the surface except in early evening; they have great difficulty in moving.

Thread Snake

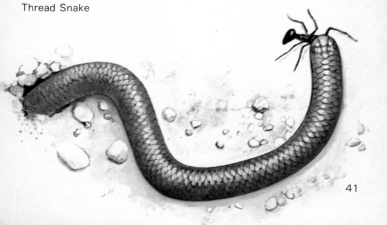

Anilidae

Another small family of burrowing snakes includes the false coral snake and the pipe snakes. Found in southeast Asia and South America, they still have vestiges of hind limbs showing as claws but have developed small belly shields on the underside. They still have two lungs, although the left one is very tiny; the eyes have a spectacle covering.

Some authorities consider the pipe snakes to be in some ways intermediate between the shieldtails and boas, for they have a very solid skull like the former group. In spite of this, some species take quite large pieces of food such as eels and other snakes, which may be a foot long—as long as the snake itself. Among the Anilidae are one or two interesting cases of what may be mimicry. The South American false coral snake's vivid colors are similar to those of a poisonous coral snake found in the same region, and it may gain protection from this. The pipe snake of Malaya, if it is frightened, flattens itself, lifts its tail to show the crimson underside and waves it over its body. This performance may look sufficiently like a threatening head to deter aggressors.

Malayan Pipe Snake

Xenopeltidae

The sunbeam snake (*Xenopeltis unicolor*) has no very close relations and is put in a family by itself, although some zoologists would include the aberrant python *Loxocemus* in the same family. *Loxocemus* lives in Mexico, far removed from all other pythons; it has some features in common with the sunbeam snake, although its external appearance is that of a python.

The sunbeam snake has two lungs, although one is bigger

Sunbeam Snake

than the other, but no trace of limbs or pelvis. The head is small but has typical shields covering it, immobile jaws, and a solid compact skull for pushing into earth. It lives in southeast Asia, grows to three feet long, and spends much of its time burrowing. As it is nocturnal, the sunbeam snake is seldom seen. The color of this snake is dull but if seen in certain lights the shiny scales provide a brilliant iridescence that gives the snake its common name. The main food is frogs, snakes, and lizards.

Loxocemus

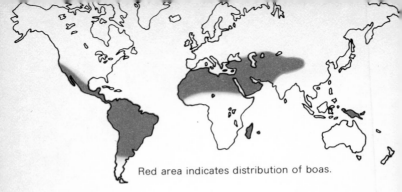

Red area indicates distribution of boas.

THE BOIDAE

This family includes the giants among living snakes. Boas and pythons show features that mark them off from the majority of living snakes as being more primitive, with bodies less changed from the lizard pattern. They have a recognizable pelvic girdle and hind limbs, although these are vestigial and do not help the snake move. The pelvic girdle has the same bones as that of a lizard but is tiny and not attached to the backbone. The two legs are tiny single bones, each covered by a horny claw that can be seen projecting from the snake's body in front of the cloaca. In females, the claws seem functionless; males use them to stroke the females' flanks during courtship.

Boas and pythons have two functional lungs, with the right lung larger than the left. Like some of the primitive burrowing snakes, the Boidae have a small remnant of a coronoid bone in their lower jaw. In lizards this bone is important and helps to keep the jaw rigid, but in most snakes it is absent, aiding jaw flexibility.

As in many bulky snakes, there is a tendency to move by rectilinear creeping. The boas and pythons that climb have a tail that is extremely prehensile, a useful characteristic for a relatively heavy snake.

None of the Boidae are poisonous and all kill their prey by constriction. The snake strikes at its victim, seizing it with its large backward-pointing teeth, then coiling its body round that of the prey. Often the snake keeps hold of a fixed object with its tail to enable it to get some purchase on the animal it intends to overpower. Once coiled around, it hangs on and squeezes until the victim succumbs. The prey is never crushed to death, or even noticeably deformed before it is eaten. Death comes by suffocation, the victim being unable to move its ribs and breathe while it is being constricted.

A snake will swallow its prey whole. The story that the large constrictors first crush their prey shapeless and then lick it all over before swallowing is false; it has probably arisen because pythons that have recently been fed and are then surprised may disgorge their food before escaping. The food is by that stage already partly digested and therefore covered with mucus.

The Boas
The true boas are found mostly in the Americas where there are over thirty species, but there are about ten burrowing types in Western Asia and adjacent parts of North Africa. There are three species of boa on Madagascar and five species inhabiting Pacific Islands.

Boas differ from pythons in that they bear living young; there are also small differences in skull bones.

Boa Skull

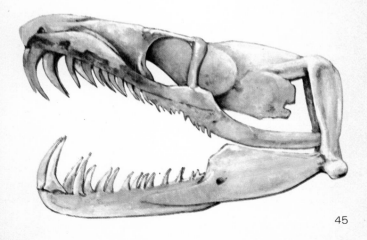

The Boa Constrictor (*Constrictor constrictor*) has a large range and is found from Mexico in Central America to the central parts of Argentina. It is able to thrive under extremely diverse conditions, some specimens living in tropical rain forests and others inhabiting arid lands.

The name boa constrictor is sometimes used in popular language for any of the giant constricting snakes, and imagination has often endowed it with huge size and strange habits. In fact, the true boa constrictor is not the largest snake in the world. It ranks fifth in maximum size and must even cede first place in its native South America to the anaconda. The maximum size ever recorded has been 18½ feet, but the average is several feet less than this.

Most of the really large boa constrictors seem to live in Central America; in this area, the markings are less handsome, being darker and less well defined, than in the South American type. Central American specimens are said to have an irascible temperament, hissing loudly and striking repeatedly if disturbed, while South American boa constrictors become tame fairly readily. Wild boa constrictors may harbor ticks on their bodies; the heavy infestation found in many Central American examples may partly explain their irritability.

Boa constrictors' food is varied, but warm-blooded animals are eaten more often than cold-blooded. Rodents are the usual food, but mammals as large as ocelots may be consumed. Boa constrictors also eat some birds and the larger kinds of lizard. They are known to have lived for 23 years in captivity.

The Rainbow Boa (*Epicrates cenchris*) lives in areas from Costa Rica to Argentina, over roughly the same range as the boa constrictor. It is a slow-moving snake that rarely grows to a length of more than four feet. This snake is not named because of its body colors, which are a dull mixture of browns and black relieved with a little white. In sunlight, however, the structure of the scales gives rise to interference colors in the way a thin film of oil on water does, so that the snake has a shimmering iridescence appearing to be colored in bright green and blue. The scales of all snakes of the genus *Epicrates* have this iridescence, but it is seen at its best in the rainbow boa.

Although it spends much time on the ground, the rainbow boa is a good climber with a fairly prehensile tail. As well as eating rodents captured on the ground, it sometimes ascends trees and catches bats. Like the Cuban boa (see page 50), it has lip pits.

Rainbow Boa

The Rubber Boa *(Charina bottae)* is a North American species found in the western United States; its range even extends a little into southwest Canada, where it is found in damp coniferous forests. It is a small boa, averaging only 18 inches in length, and the last few tail vertebrae are solidly fused. Because of its color, it is sometimes known as the silver boa. This snake spends much of its time burrowing and it has the blunt head and tail usual among burrowing snakes. It feeds mostly on small rodents and mammals, and is of gentle disposition toward humans.

When the rubber boa is threatened, it has a characteristic defense reaction that consists of curling itself into a tight ball. Usually the tail is left outside the ball, and this is raised over the snake and moved back and forth in a way reminiscent of an ordinary snake striking with its head. By exposing the least important and vulnerable part of its anatomy in this way, the rubber boa can quite effectively scare off uninitiated foes.

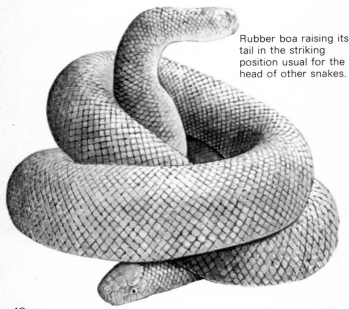

Rubber boa raising its tail in the striking position usual for the head of other snakes.

Tree Boa

The Emerald Tree Boa *(Boa canina)* is found in tropical South America. As its name suggests, it is arboreal and it has an extremely prehensile tail. It feeds mainly on birds and squirrels, and also on iguana lizards. It possesses front teeth that are highly developed, probably proportionately larger than those of any other non-venomous snake. Tree boas grow to about six feet.

When adult, emerald tree boas are a bright emerald green with creamy or white spots. These boas rest in a characteristically coiled position on the top of branches, with the front of the body above and inside the outer rings, looking a little like a bunch of green bananas. The color, posture, and the light spots break up the outline of the snake's body, leaving them almost impossible to detect at rest in the trees. Although the adults are this uniform and striking color, the young specimens are more variable and differ from their parents. They are yellowish, or even pink, with white markings edged with dark purple or green. As they become mature, the markings change to the adult pattern. In captivity, emerald tree boas are usually quiet and can be handled without attempting to bite.

49

Cuban Boa

The Cuban Boa *(Epicrates angulifer)* is found on Cuba and the Isle of Pines and is the largest of the Cuban snakes, growing to a little over ten feet in length. Early in this century, some of these boas were reported to have reached fourteen feet in length; large specimens are now rare, although the species still flourishes in the wilder areas of the island. When individual boas come into contact with man, as for instance in sugar cane plantations, they are liable to be needlessly killed even when they might be beneficial for the control of rodents. The greater part of the diet of the Cuban boa is, however, made up of bats. Like its prey, it is largely nocturnal and has sensory pits in its lips which appear to function as heat detectors. Labial pits of this type are found in many of the Boidae but are not common to all; the boa constrictor, for example, does not have them. As might be expected, heat detectors are of most use to a snake hunting warm-blooded prey after dark, when eyes cannot function so efficiently (see p. 130).

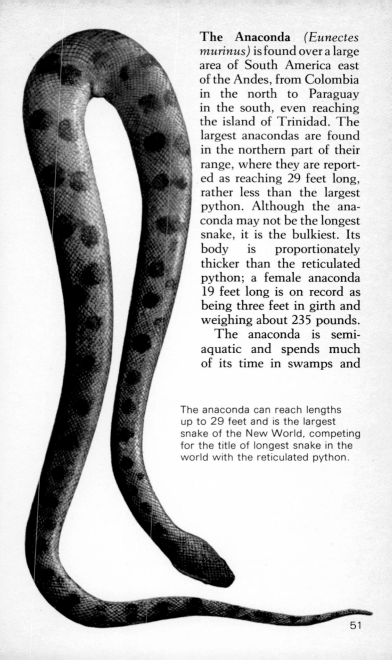

The Anaconda *(Eunectes murinus)* is found over a large area of South America east of the Andes, from Colombia in the north to Paraguay in the south, even reaching the island of Trinidad. The largest anacondas are found in the northern part of their range, where they are reported as reaching 29 feet long, rather less than the largest python. Although the anaconda may not be the longest snake, it is the bulkiest. Its body is proportionately thicker than the reticulated python; a female anaconda 19 feet long is on record as being three feet in girth and weighing about 235 pounds.

The anaconda is semi-aquatic and spends much of its time in swamps and

The anaconda can reach lengths up to 29 feet and is the largest snake of the New World, competing for the title of longest snake in the world with the reticulated python.

slow-moving rivers, although it is not an especially good swimmer. It eats few fish, preferring to lie in wait near the edge of the water with just the eyes and nostrils above water, ready to capture birds and mammals coming down to drink. The anaconda's bill of fare is extensive: waterfowl, rodents such as agoutis, coypus and capybaras, the occasional cayman, and mammals up to the size of peccaries and young tapirs. Anacondas have also been known to have eaten dogs, sheep, and pigs. If they are disturbed by humans, anacondas usually make for water, where they are able to submerge for over ten minutes.

Like the other boas, anacondas are ovoviviparous. The 19-foot female mentioned previously gave birth to 72 young, each three feet long and an inch in girth.

There are seven species of small boa that live in the Old World and are known as sand boas. None grows longer than three feet, and they mostly live in dry sandy country in the Middle East and North Africa; one species extends eastward north of the Himalayas to northwest China, and one extends south of the Himalayas to northeast India. The sand boas are burrowing animals, equipped with narrow valvular nostrils to keep sand out of their nose; they have an enlarged scale on their snout that probably helps them to dig. Although small, the sand boas tend to be aggressive, delivering sideways slashing bites.

The Brown Sand Boa *(Eryx johni)* is an Indian species growing two and a half feet long, with blunt tail, very small eyes, and tiny scales. It often assumes a coiled-up position with its tail sticking out.

The Brown Sand Boa

Sanzinia

Three species of boa live on Madagascar. One of them, *Sanzinia madagascariensis*, grows to seven feet long and is mainly arboreal, like the New World tree boas that it resembles. Like them, too, it has marked labial pits.

On Round Island (near Mauritius in the Indian Ocean) live two species of boa *(Casarea dussumiere* and *Bolyeria multicarinata)*. Not only are these isolated by many miles of sea from other boas, but they are peculiar in that they lack any vestige of hind limbs or pelvic girdle; they also have a much smaller left lung than typical members of the boa family. They are usually placed in a subfamily of their own (Bolyerinae) because of these and other differences. These boas may be some form of link between boas and some of the other groups of snakes.

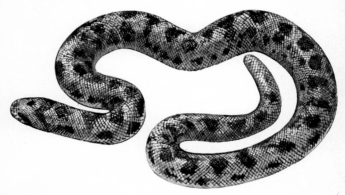
Round Island Boa

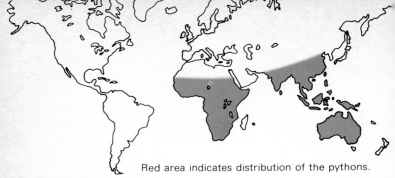
Red area indicates distribution of the pythons.

The Pythons

Pythons differ from boas in that they have an extra pair of bones, called supraorbitals, in their skull roof, and also in that they lay eggs rather than produce living young. Although some authorities place them in a separate family, we have chosen to consider them as a subfamily, Pythoninae, within the family of the Boidae. The distribution of the snakes in the Pythoninae subfamily is reasonably widespread and they can be found in Africa, southeast Asia, Malaysia, and the Philippines. Even in some of the Pacific islands and in Australia there are a few scattered species.

Many fallacies exist over the tremendous amount of strength that a python can be credited with. There is a belief that a human who encounters a python in the wild may be squeezed to death by the snake. In fact, the snake will usually defend itself by striking, the same manner in which all other snakes do. The crushing power relies on the suffocation principle employed by many snakes and described in detail previously (see page 45).

The Pythoninae vary greatly in length. The reticulated python can reach a size of over 30 feet at its greatest length; the Indian python *(Python molurus)* will often exceed twenty feet. Alternatively, there are pythons of a small size; the royal python of Africa, for example, has an average length of only three feet.

The Reticulated Python *(Python reticulatus)* is found in southeast Asia, from Thailand southward to the Malay Archipelago and the Philippine Islands. The maximum authenticated length is about 32 feet, and it is probably the longest of the world's snakes, although it is certainly not the most heavily built of snakes.

The reticulated python is usually found near water in the wild, but it has also been known to frequent areas where there is much human activity. It was said to be common even in busy parts of Bangkok early in the twentieth century; although it sometimes made itself a nuisance eating domestic animals, it probably helped to keep down the rats. Although it is large enough on occasion to prey on wild pigs, the reticulated python eats mostly small mammals.

This snake is not normally considered dangerous to man: although a large specimen is powerful enough to kill a human, it would probably be unable to work its head over the shoulders of an adult. Occasionally, however, a person is attacked, and there is a record from Indonesia of a 14-year-old boy being eaten by a reticulated python.

The reticulated python lays between 10 and 100 eggs; after an incubation period of 8 to 11 weeks, the young are hatched. They start life with a length of at least two feet.

Sometimes called the Asiatic Rock Python, the **Indian Python** *(Python molurus)*, is the common python of southern Asia, occuring from West Pakistan in the west, to southern China in the east and southward to the Malay Archipelago. Like the reticulated python, it is often found near

Reticulated python, probably the longest of the world's snakes.

water, or even in it, where it can remain submerged for half an hour or more. It is a good climber and can hang from a tree by its prehensile tail. In this pose, it stays still and waits, striking at any potential victim that comes within range. It is not such a long snake as the reticulated python, reaching a maximum of about 20 feet, but it is much more heavily built and usually more sluggish in its movements.

The Indian python also eats larger prey, normally warm-blooded, and has even been known to kill and eat a leopard. The python that accomplished this was 18 feet long, and its meal was four feet long, excluding tail. The Indian python rarely attacks man unless provoked, but there is a record of a Chinese baby living near Hong Kong being eaten.

Indian python preying on a leopard.

Blood Python

Probably many more of these pythons have been eaten by people than vice versa as they are regarded as being very good meat in some parts of the world and they are so sluggish they hardly ever try to escape. Westerners who have tasted them have usually pronounced them to be palatable. Pythons are not often thought of as hibernating animals, but in colder parts of their range, such as North India, Indian pythons rest for several months every year. But it is not true hibernation, as mating seems to take place at this time.

Subsequently the female python makes a shallow nest and lays her eggs, which may be as many as 100, the maximum known clutch being 107. The mother coils around the nest and remains two months or more without feeding until the eggs hatch and the baby pythons emerge. The babies are about two feet six inches when they hatch and grow rapidly. It is possible for them to reach six and a half feet after a year and over nine feet after two years if conditions are favorable. In one case, the newly hatched snakes were observed to crawl back at night into their empty shells, which were still guarded by the mother. The Indian python is normally docile in captivity, but big specimens may become dangerous to handle.

Much smaller than the reticulated or Indian python, the **Blood Python** *(Python curtus)* grows to a maximum of only nine feet. Like its two relatives, it is fond of water and can be found almost exclusively in, or by, rivers and streams where it makes a living feeding on the rats and mice that are common there. The blood python lives in Malaya and the Malay Archipelago.

The Ball Python *(Python regius)* lives in equatorial West Africa and can reach a length of five feet, although its average length is about three feet. Its small size and gentle nature make it one of the most suitable snakes to keep as a pet.

When a ball python is frightened in the wild, it will curl

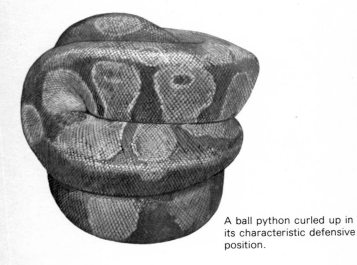

A ball python curled up in its characteristic defensive position.

itself into a tight ball with the head on the inside, a habit reminiscent of the rubber boa, and also sometimes found in the blood python. When coiled, a ball python is almost perfectly spherical and can be rolled for many feet. In captivity, this trick can unfortunately rarely be carried out as the python becomes too tame to react.

The Green Tree Python *(Chondropython viridis)*, sometimes known as the Papuan Tree Python, is found in New

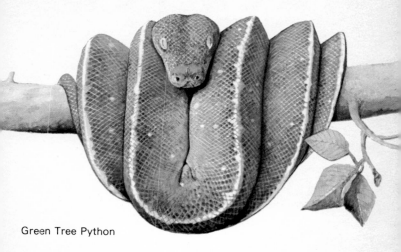

Green Tree Python

Guinea and is leaf-green in color. It is remarkable in showing great similarities to the emerald tree boa.

The adult snakes of both species are emerald green with white or cream markings; at a glance, it would be difficult to tell the two apart. Even the resting postures, looped over a branch, are similar.

As with the emerald tree boa, the young are a different color from the adults, usually brick-red; as they grow, they turn first yellow, then green.

This New Guinea python further resembles the American tree boa in being specially adapted to a life in the treetops. It has enlarged front teeth, their great length enabling them to more easily catch moving prey. Both these snakes also have a well-developed prehensile tail. There is perhaps no better example of two animals coming to look alike than these two snakes, not because they are especially closely related, but because they have both become adapted to living in the same way under similar conditions.

The green tree python grows to an average of seven feet long. It is a beautiful snake but it is rarely found in museum collections or in zoological gardens in any great numbers.

The Diamond Python *(Morelia argus)* is found in Australia and New Guinea. (It was known as *Python spilotes* for a long time, but can now be distinguished as a closely related genus *Morelia*.) Its species name, *argus*, refers to the bright yellow spots on each scale.

There are, in fact, two color varieties. One is light brown with dark brown markings; the other is bluish-black with the little yellow spots previously described and also larger diamond-shaped yellow markings that give the snake its name. The former variety is sometimes called the carpet snake or carpet python and the color is much closer to that of the other pythons.

Only exceptionally is an individual more than 10 feet long, although diamond pythons over 14 feet have been recorded. Like most of the pythons, the diamond python is at home in the water but is not found exclusively near it. It can also climb well and has a prehensile tail. It consumes small mammals and is occasionally introduced into barns to control rodents.

Diamond Python

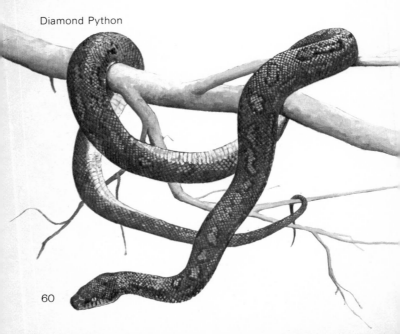

Calabar Ground Python

The Calabar Ground Python *(Calabaria reinhardti)* is a small burrower found in the rain forests of West and Central Africa, from Liberia throughout the Congo. It grows only a little longer than three feet and spends much of its time burrowing underground or moving through the dead leaves of the forest floor searching for its prey, small mammals such as shrews and mice.

This little snake parallels the rubber boa in its habits, even extending the resemblance to its defense-reaction, which is to curl up into a motionless ball. The Calabar ground python has a cylindrical body and smooth scales, as well as the blunt head with reduced head shields and the short-tail characteristic of burrowers.

One peculiarity of this snake is that, as it moves around on the ground, it keeps its head pointed down; at the same time, it keeps its tail up and moves this back and forth in a way reminiscent of the head movements of more normal snakes. This device presumably gives some protection from attack to the head. It at least protects the snake from some of the natives of its home region, who keep well away from it because they believe it has two heads.

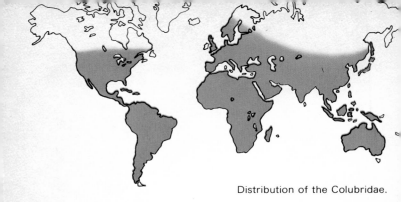

Distribution of the Colubridae.

THE COLUBRIDAE

Almost three-quarters of the genera of snakes in the world, and over three-quarters of the species, belong to the family Colubridae. Colubrids are the typical common snakes of all the continents of the world except for Australia, where the cobra family predominate. They live in a variety of habitats, —on the ground, in trees, or in the water. Some specialize in one of these habitats, but many move with ease in all three. Their food-gathering methods are rarely uniform; some are constrictors and many swallow their food with no preliminaries. Most colubrids are completely harmless to man, although their saliva may be toxic to their prey. They have no fangs or true venom. The exceptions to this, a few small groups or subfamilies such as the Boiginae, are dealt with later.

In the colubrid snakes, there is only one lung and never any sign of limbs or pelvis. There is nearly always a single row of belly-shields or scales, each corresponding with a single vertebra. The upper part of the head is covered with enlarged scales, and there are typically nine of these shields. The lower jaw has only two bones on each side and both jaws are highly mobile and distensible; the braincase is the only rigid part of the skull. There is a fold in the skin of the lower jaw to allow for stretching during feeding. Most of the Colubridae belong to the subfamily Colubrinae, which includes such familiar snakes as the watersnakes, garter snakes, and racers.

Colubrinae

The Northern Watersnake *(Natrix sipedon)* is one of 11 relatively common species of watersnakes to be found in North America. Most of these species are confined to the eastern half of the United States, but some of them range up into southeastern Canada, while others are found down in Mexico and even in Guatemala. Only one species is found west of the Rocky Mountains, and this one is confined to Lower California and Mexico's Pacific coastal region.

As their names suggest, all these snakes live in and about ponds, lakes, swamps, streams, rivers—wherever there is fresh water. They seem to prefer quiet waters, although watersnakes may also be found near waterfalls and swift-flowing water. Their principal diet is, obviously, dictated by their habitat, and includes fishes, frogs, tadpoles, crayfish, and salamanders; some species will also prey on birds or other small animals. Incidentally, although they eat their share of fishes, they tend not to go for the kinds that in-

terest human fishers, and so these snakes can hardly be considered even competitors, let alone enemies, of man. However, they can be extremely aggressive; and although their bite is not poisonous, there can be considerable bleeding if a watersnake gets its fangs into a limb. Furthermore, a bite can be painful—and troublesome, if an infection develops.

The particular species singled out here is found from Maine (and occasionally in Quebec, Canada), south as far as North Carolina and across the southern uplands, and west as far as Colorado. Its range overlaps that of several other watersnakes, and it can easily be confused with certain of them such as the banded watersnake, the blotched watersnake, or the northern copperbelly. But the northern watersnake can usually be distinguished by its bright coloration:

dark crossbands on its neck and foreparts; alternating dorsal and lateral blotches on the rest of the body; black or reddish half-moons on the belly. Its ground color varies from gray to dark brown; its markings from black to reddish-brown. As do virtually all the species of American watersnakes, the adults of the northern watersnake tend to get darker as they age; the distinctive pattern is obscured so that an adult may, in fact, appear to be a plain dark brown or black snake. Anyone determined to identify the species could place the snake under water, where the pattern would usually reveal itself.

The watersnakes of America are ovoviviparous, giving birth to from 6 to 58 young; this is in contrast, by the way, to the watersnakes of the Old World, which are oviparous and which give birth usually to more eggs. There are about 75 species of watersnakes found throughout the world, making them one of the most numerous and widespread groups of non-poisonous snakes.

Although they lack poison, the watersnakes have ingenious ways of defending themselves. When molested—by man or by other enemies—they will first attempt to escape by diving and swimming away. Cornered, however, various watersnakes will inflate their bodies with air, hiss loudly, flatten their heads, and then strike. The common watersnake *(Natrix natrix)* of Europe, North Africa, and points eastward into Central Asia is even reported as turning over on its back, with mouth open and tongue lolling—mimicking a dead snake in behavior reminiscent of various other snakes (see p. 76). The watersnake still has one last defense of its own: if grasped by an enemy, it will discharge the contents of its anal glands, a non-poisonous but foul-smelling secretion.

Although a good swimmer and dependent on various water animals for much of its diet, the northern watersnake spends much of its time basking on overhanging branches (or on shores).

Perhaps the most widespread species of watersnake in the Old World is the *Natrix natrix,* which occurs over most of Europe, parts of North Africa, and eastward to Central Asia. It has many local names, being best known in England as the grass snake. But since we have already pictured this species—see the illustration on page 28—and since its habits do not differ greatly from the watersnakes of North America, we shall examine a different Old World watersnake as a representative of this widespread group.

The Viperine Watersnake *(Natrix maura)* is a close relative of the common European watersnake also found in the western Mediterranean area. The viperine watersnake is present in France, Spain, and northwest Italy, as well as northwest Africa and some of the Mediterranean islands such as Corsica and Sardinia.

The viperine watersnake is nearly always found in the neighborhood of water; the still waters of marshes and ponds are the preferred habitat. The snake may be in the water or nearby hiding under a branch or stone; when disturbed, it will head for the water. Sometimes ponds can be found where large numbers of snakes have congregated on the banks, only to dive in when approached.

Much of the food is caught in the water and this consists of frogs, fish, and salamanders, although there are occasional lesser fare, such as earthworms. As in the common European watersnake, the female is larger than the male and grows to over three feet.

Viperine Water Snakes

Eastern Garter Snake

The Eastern Garter Snake (*Thamnophis sirtalis*) is merely one species of the most common snake genus of North America, the garter snakes. They are not only the most numerous and most widely distributed snakes but, for most people, they are 'a snake.' They have persisted in making their homes in meadows, hillsides, forests, marshlands, and gardens, even as man has moved closer and closer with his towns and roads. For the average urban dweller, when he chances upon a snake in a vacant lot, a drainage ditch, or a backyard, the odds are it is some species of garter snake.

The eastern garter snake has a range from southeastern Canada, across the eastern part of the United States to the Gulf of Mexico, and west as far as Minnesota and eastern Texas. Although there are various other garter snakes in this range, the eastern garter snake is to be distinguished as the only one that has lateral stripes confined to the second and third rows; the other garter snakes within the range have stripes along a fourth row. Beyond this, however, the eastern garter snake varies greatly in its coloration and pattern. The ground color may be black, dark brown, green, or olive; the stripes are usually yellow, but may be brown, green, or even bluish; usually there is a double row of alternating black spots between the spots. Either spots or stripes may predominate; some specimens will have almost no signs of stripes; and completely black, or melanistic, specimens are occasionally reported.

The eastern garter snake mates in April or May; the young are born alive about three months later. Brood size is about 25, but a maximum of 78 has been recorded. The young are five to nine inches at birth; an adult grows to about two feet in length, although the record is reported for an Ohio specimen three feet eight inches long.

Garter snakes feed on earthworms, insects, toads, salamanders, and occasionally on small mammals or birds. But a large part of their diet includes aquatic creatures—fishes, crayfishes, frogs—and, in general, garter snakes seem to prefer to live near water, or at least on damp ground. In the western part of their American range, which is more arid, garter snakes are virtually restricted to habitats near water sources. This predilection for water has led to their being popularly called 'watersnakes,' but although they are related to the true watersnakes, they should not be confused with them. Like the true watersnakes, garter snakes, when captured, may eject a foul liquid from their anal glands. If handled—and fed—properly, garter snakes are docile enough to do well in captivity.

There are so many garter snakes of the genus *Thamnophis* that it is hard to single out any. (Their common name, 'garter,' in case you are still wondering, is derived from the striped elastic garters that men once used for holding up their socks.) But we might at least depict one more—and one of the most colorful, the San Francisco garter snake (*Thamnophis sirtalis tetrataenia*); its dashing red stripes prove that even the common garter snake can be a handsome creature.

San Francisco Garter Snake

The Corn Snake *(Elaphe guttata),* or red rat snake, is found in the southeastern United States. It is nocturnal, equally at home climbing or on the ground, and may be found in the open or in woods. Like most of its relatives, it is a constrictor and it coils around its prey exceptionally fast. The food includes rats and small birds such as quail. The corn snake averages three feet long with a maximum of six feet.

The American snakes of the genus *Elaphe* are often known

Corn Snake

as 'rat snakes' or 'chicken snakes' because of their diet. They are generally useful predators on rodents but occasionally wreak havoc with chicken flocks.

The Black Rat Snake *(Elaphe obsoleta)* is a large but harmless constrictor. The average adult size is four feet long, but some specimens have been collected over eight feet in length. This snake is also known as the pilot black snake because it lives in the same areas as copperhead snakes and is alleged to lead these to safety if danger threatens.

The black rat snake is found in the northeast United States, generally in woods or on rocky hillsides. It eats a variety of food including small birds and their eggs, mice, small rabbits, opossums, and lizards. Like most rat snakes, the black rat snake is partly arboreal. Occasional specimens have been seen more than 20 feet up in trees. The black

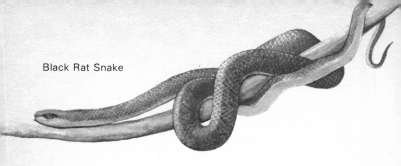

Black Rat Snake

rat snake mates in May and lays a dozen or more eggs in July, often in a pile of manure, which probably helps incubation. The young hatch about September and are just over a foot long.

The Aesculapian Snake *(Elaphe longissima),* a constrictor, is a native of southeastern Europe and Asia Minor. An average adult grows to five feet long and feeds on mice and rats, although the young snakes feed on lizards. The Aesculapian snake is a good climber but moves slowly on the ground. It lives in sparse woodland and can sometimes be found sunning itself on stones or on old stone walls. It also enters farm buildings in search of meals.

It is now accepted that this snake was the one identified with the snake symbol of the Greek god of medicine, Aesculapius; because of this association the Aesculapian snake has enjoyed protection. It has been spread by human agency to many places where it is probably not native. To the Romans, as to the Greeks, it was a symbol of health and they took the Aesculapian snake with them to the baths and spas of their colonies. Although the Romans eventually left, the

Aesculapian Snake

Leopard Snake

snakes stayed and they are still found around some modern health resorts. There are isolated populations in Switzerland and in Germany; they were found at one time in Denmark, but their northerly limit is now southern Germany.

The Leopard Snake *(Elaphe situla)* is found in southern Italy, the Balkans, many of the islands in the Mediterranean, Turkey, and the Caucasus. It grows to three and a half feet long and emerges late from hibernation, apparently waiting until the weather is really warm. This snake is found in barren rocky country and may be seen basking on walls. It is a good climber and is frequently seen in bushes, although mice are the main food. The leopard snake is a constricting snake and an egg-layer.

The Four-Lined Snake *(Elaphe quatorlineata)* is one of the largest European snakes, sometimes growing to six feet long. It can be found in the Balkan peninsula, Italy, Sicily and some of the Aegean islands, and from Turkey west to the Caucasus. It lives in woody places and among rocks and is a good climber, feeding on mice, squirrels, rats, and small birds; it also swallows small eggs whole.

The snake lays quite large eggs, which hatch into nine-inch youngsters. The four-lined snake is not aggressive and rarely bites.

Four-Lined Snake

71

Northern Black Racer

The Northern Black Racer *(Coluber constrictor),* also known as an eastern racer, is one of several species of long, slender snakes reputed to be extremely swift. Most of the members of the genus *Coluber* are to be found across Asia, southern Europe, and North Africa, but the northern black racer is one of several racers found in the New World. They range from southern Canada down through into Middle America.

The northern black racer is a dark blue-black—both below as well as above—with whitish chin and throat. The young are more strongly patterned, as the adults tend to darken with age. Adults average about four feet in length, and their slenderness, combined with their coloring, gives them an appearance of a satin streak. The racers of the American West are smaller, and are green-brown or yellow-brown in color. There is also a speckled form, the tropic racer, found only in the southern part of Texas.

Racers feed mainly on small mammals, birds, frogs, lizards, and even other snakes. They seem to be as much at home in the branches of bushes and trees as on the ground; when approached, they are apt to flee into branches.

Now, like most snakes, they will usually flee when approached, and there is no denying that they move remarkably fast across all kinds of terrain. But there is serious doubt among authorities if they really move as fast as popular stories claim. As we have mentioned (see page 17), snakes cannot and do not move all that fast, for a number of reasons. The most reliable tests of the fast snakes such as the racers and whip snakes has produced speed of only about three and a half miles an hour.

What really distinguishes a snake such as the racer, however, is its fiercely defensive behavior when cornered or grasped. Some racers, for instance, will vibrate the tip of their tails, producing a sound in dry vegetation that could lead an attacker to think it is a rattlesnake. If grasped firmly by the neck, racers lash their dangling bodies back and forth vigorously. And if they do get a chance to bite, they will jerk their head to one side, ripping the skin with their sharp jaws; others have been reported as taking several quick bites in rapid succession. So although neither poisonous nor supernaturally swift, racers are certainly worthy opponents.

The European Whip Snake *(Coluber gemonensis)* is found from western Europe to the Caucasus, and is especially common in Italy and parts of the Balkans. It can grow to six feet or more but most are considerably smaller. It is an active snake and is a good climber frequenting shrubs and woodland, preying on nestlings as well as running down prey on the ground. Its favorite food is lizards and other snakes, but it will eat voles and also insects such as locusts.

European Whip Snake

Coachwhip Snake

The Coachwhip Snake *(Masticophis flagellum)* is found a-
cross the southern United States and in Mexico. It is found
mostly in dry open country, although it climbs well and may
be encountered in bushes or down on the ground. The
coachwhip snake derives its name from the legend that it
would attack people, bind the victim to a tree with its coils,
and then whip him to death with its tail. There is, of course,
no truth in this. It is not even a constricting snake, and,
with a normal adult length of about four feet, it is much too
small to accomplish this feat. Like other snakes, the coachwhip vibrates its tail when annoyed. Occasionally larger
specimens of up to eight feet are found, but even these
could not bind or whip a man.

The only grain of truth in the story lies, perhaps, in the
fact that coachwhip snakes readily attack if approached.
They strike, bite, then relax the forepart of the body for a
moment, only to jerk it straight and make a tearing wound.
Being diurnal, they are fairly commonly seen. Their prey,
which they grab and swallow, ranges from insects to rattlesnakes, small mammals and especially lizards. They mate
in spring, and the female lays about eight, rough-surfaced
eggs.

The Smooth Green Snake *(Opheodrys vernalis)* is a small
snake found in the United States and southern Canada;
15 inches is a good size for a specimen. It is quite a common
snake, but because of its size and color is fairly inconspic-
uous. It is usually found in fields and marshes, where it
feeds on spiders and insects.

A small number of eggs are laid in July or August; as
most of the development has taken place before the eggs

are laid, it is generally only a few days before the young hatch out, measuring about four and a half inches.

The genus *Pituophis* contains several species known collectively as **Bull Snakes.** All the bull snakes have the scale at the tip of the snout enlarged upward on the head, a modification for their partly burrowing habits.

Pituophis catenifer is found in the Pacific region of America in all sorts of habitats except high mountains. An average adult is four and a half feet in length. The species *Pituophis catenifer* is also often called the gopher snake, as it includes pocket gophers in its diet. The eastern form of the bull snake is usually known as a pine snake.

The bull snakes are popular with farmers because of the work they do in keeping rodents in check. One adult gopher snake was found with 35 small mice inside it. As well as mice and gophers, they eat rabbits and ground squirrels.

Bull snakes are notable for their hissing. They have a special membrane in front of the entrance to their windpipe. When they are annoyed and hiss, the membrane vibrates, giving a hoarse rhythmic effect to the loud hiss.

Bull or Gopher, Snake

75

The Indigo Snake *(Drymarchon corais)* ranges from Brazil to the gulf states of the United States and occurs in several varieties. The usual color in the United States is a deep blue-black, from which the snake gets its name, and the smooth glossy scales which may show iridescence. The habits of the wild indigo snake are not well known, but it is often found in the burrows of gopher tortoises and for this reason it is sometimes called the 'blue gopher.' It does well in captivity, rarely biting, and eating almost anything of suitable size. The indigo snake does not constrict its prey, and captured specimens have disgorged other snakes. The longest recorded indigo snake was seven feet nine inches in length, which makes this snake one of the largest non-venomous North American snakes. The average is about five feet long. The indigo snake is oviparous.

The Hog-nosed Snake *(Heterodon platyrhinos)* is a small snake about two feet in length; it gets its name from its upturned snout, which, like a pig's nose, is used for digging in earth. The skull also is built for burrowing; as the snake burrows, it arches its neck and pushes its head into the earth. Toads, probably encountered as the snake burrows, are eaten and also other amphibians and insects. The hog-nosed snake is found in the dry, eastern United States; relatives are found in the south and farther west.

The hog-nosed snake is chiefly of interest because of its defensive behavior. If it is molested, it first spreads its head, neck, and foreparts to twice their normal width, fills its lungs,

A hog-nosed snake playing dead.

then gives vent to a loud hiss. (Such behavior has earned it such common names as 'puff adder' or 'blow snake.') Following this, it strikes at its foe, although usually with closed mouth. If all this display fails, the snake suddenly changes its tactics and starts rolling around as though in agony, contorting and rubbing the open mouth in the dirt. Then the snake turns on its back and lies still, apparently dead, even to the extent of being completely limp if picked up. No doubt this performance is often sufficient to save it from further attack. The only thing that mars the performance is that, if a hog-nosed snake on its back is turned right way up, it immediately rolls upside down again.

The King Snake *(Lampropeltis getulus)* is found in the eastern United States mostly in the dry pine forest areas, although the snake itself likes the water and is often found near streams. The king snake is generally between three and four feet long, although a maximum of five feet eight inches has been recorded. It is not seen very commonly as it is shy, hiding under logs or stones, and largely nocturnal. If caught, the king snake, like its relatives, can be vicious, biting and chewing hard. After a time in captivity, they usually become quite good-natured.

In many places, the king snake is protected because of its snake-eating habits. The king snake eats some mammals, lizards and even turtle eggs; but most of its food consists of other snakes, many poisonous, so it is considered very useful. It is adept at constriction.

The Milk Snake *(Lampropeltis doliata)* is another member of the king snake genus and lives in the eastern United States and southeastern Canada. It is about two and a half feet long and is secretive and nocturnal; although occasionally seen basking in the day, it is normally necessary to search in rotten tree stumps or under logs to find it. Like the other king snakes, it is vicious if cornered; when aroused, it vibrates its tail.

Unlike most king snakes, the milk snake is not primarily a snake-eater. Most of the diet takes the form of small mammals. Other food includes slugs, birds, and a few snakes.

The milk snake lays its eggs in manure heaps in June or July, thirteen being the average number. The name is acquired from the belief that this snake drank from cows, but there appears to be no truth in this, and it will always drink water in preference to milk when both are available.

King snake
constricting
a copperhead

The **Leaf-nosed Snakes** of the *Phyllorhynchus* species are so named because the rostral shield—the scale at the tip of the snout—is enlarged and flattened, presumably for use as a burrowing organ. Leaf-nosed snakes are found in Mexico and the southwestern United States. They are desert dwellers, spending most days underground and only emerging and moving around at night. Their nocturnal habits for a long time had zoologists fooled, for leaf-nosed snakes were discovered in 1868 and were thought to be very rare; only ten were found in the next 50 years. Then suddenly it was discovered by L. Klauber, a native of San Diego, that it was possible to collect dozens of these snakes by driving along desert roads at night and spotting the snakes in the headlights.

The leaf-nosed snakes are, in fact, abundant where they occur. Although heavy-bodied, leaf-nosed snakes rarely exceed fifteen inches long. They feed on lizard eggs when those are available, or else on small lizards or insects. **The Western Ring-necked Snake** *(Diadophis amabilis)* is one of three species of ring-necked snakes to be found in North America. Its range, as its name suggests, is the far west of the United States—actually, a wide strip along the Pacific coast. There is an eastern ring-necked species that has a much larger range throughout the eastern half of the United States; a third species has a small range in the southwest and—like the western ring-necked snake—is also to be found in northern Mexico.

When annoyed, leaf-nosed snakes coil like rattlesnakes and strike, but their bite is not serious.

Most ring-necked snakes are easily recognized by the slate-gray coloring of their backs; the yellow, red, or orange ring—bordered in black—behind the head; and the bright underside of yellow, orange, or red.

Ring-necked snakes are small, growing to only about 15 to 20 inches, with maximum length reported as from two to three feet. They live mainly in moist woodlands or rocky wooded hillsides, and are secretive, rarely seen snakes. They spend much of their time under stones, logs, or rotting trees; there they find the insects and worms they eat, in addition to salamanders, small snakes, lizards, and frogs; there, too, they also deposit their eggs. Several individual ring-necked snakes may gather near a single log.

When disturbed or molested, a ring-necked snake will usually roll its tail and raise it upward to display the bright underside. At the same time, it keeps its head off to the side or under its coil. This seems to be another instance of a harmless snake trying to bluff its way out of trouble. If captured, though, it has one weapon—a foul-smelling secretion that can be most unpleasant.

Western Ring-necked Snake

The Cape file snake
is named from the
triangular cross-
section of its body
with its high vertebral
ridge—making it look
like a file.

We shall have to conclude our survey of the numerous Colubrid snakes by singling out three unusual species.

The Cape File Snake *(Mehelya capensis)* lives in Africa from Natal north to Tanzania. It grows to five feet long, but most adults are a foot less than this and females are larger than the males. It is nocturnal and moves slowly but it is able to prey on frogs, lizards, and snakes; its preference seems to be for the poisonous night adder. The file snake is thought by some Africans to be poisonous but is actually harmless and docile even when handled.

The False Cobra *(Cyclagras gigas)* inhabits South America and grows to six and a half feet. This egg-laying snake shows sexual dimorphism, the male and female being slightly different in appearance.

The female false cobra is pale
brown all over but the male has
a pale yellow-brown background
color superimposed with black
spots.

The Vine Snake

The false cobra gets its name from its habit, when annoyed, of rearing up and spreading its neck like a true cobra. This action makes the snake appear larger and no doubt gives it some protection.

Although this snake belongs to a non-poisonous family, it has been known to produce mild symptoms in people it has bitten. Whether this is due to some weak poison, or merely to suggestion on the part of the victim, is not yet known.

The Vine Snake *(Thelotornis kirtlandi)* lives in Africa south of the Sahara, but adaptations are paralleled by the vine snakes such as *Oxybelis aeneus* of the southeastern United States and Middle America. It is only four feet long but very slender, a good shape for climbing in the trees that are its normal home, although it is able to move fast on the ground too. In trees, the snake's color provides a perfect camouflage, and it may remain still with its foreparts suspended in space for long periods. This is one of the few snakes that readily recognizes a stationary prey. A groove extends down the snout in front of the eye, and the keyhole-shaped pupil extends forward; both adaptations enable this snake to see well in front of its head for hunting or climbing. Prey may be approached swiftly in short darts and then struck at. The vine snake nearly always hangs its head down when it is holding its victim by the nose and swallows it upward. The diet is varied, with chameleons and geckos predominating. The venom is similar to that of the boomslang.

The tongue may be yellow, vermilion, or scarlet with a black tip and it is believed to function as a lure when the snake flickers it. When threatened, the vine snake inflates its throat and foreparts, showing the skin between the scales and also emphasizing the eye-spot on the neck.

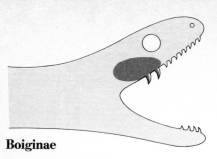

Position of the venom gland in a typical rear-fanged Boiginae snake.

Boiginae

The subfamily Boiginae is not as large as the Colubrinae, and differs from that group in its possession of a venom apparatus, although in most cases it is poorly developed. The Boiginae have one to three enlarged teeth at the back of the upper jaw, and in the surface of these teeth are grooves down which poison from the venom gland can trickle. Few of these snakes have really powerful poison, and to use their fangs they must be able to open their mouths very wide and obtain a good grip. Most of these snakes are harmless to man, although there are one or two that can be dangerous. Because they possess venom, there is no need for these snakes to be constrictors. Most of the Boiginae snakes live in tropical regions.

The Montpellier Snake *(Malpolon monspessulana)* is found in countries bordering the Mediterranean—except Italy—and its range extends eastward to Iran. It is a large snake, commonly reaching more than five feet in length and occasionally growing to six feet six inches. Although this species has large eyes and apparently good eyesight, it rarely utilizes this in climbing, usually remaining on the ground or sometimes in low bushes. It moves relatively fast and preys on small mammals, such as voles and rats, and also on such birds as it may be able to find on the ground; sometimes it catches snakes or lizards. If the prey is small, it is simply grabbed and swallowed, but larger prey is left until it is immobilized by the effect of the venom of this rear-fanged snake. Mammals of the size usually eaten by this snake die in a matter of minutes from the poison, which seems to be a nerve poison like that of many cobras. Although small mammals are easily overcome, the bite of a Montpellier snake is unlikely to have much effect on a human as the fangs lie too far back in the jaw to come into play. But there has been at least one case of a man becoming ill after being chewed by one.

In spite of being poisonous itself, the Montpellier snake is frequently preyed on by the venomous sand viper. The venom of the sand viper is of a different type from that of the Montpellier snake, and the latter seems to have little resistance to it.

The Black-and-Yellow Mangrove Snake *(Boiga dendrophila)* lives in Malaysia and the Philippines and is sometimes known as the 'tree snake.' Tree snake is an apt description of this snake, as it is completely arboreal, scarcely, if ever, descending to the ground of the forests and mangrove swamp where it lives. The black-and-yellow mangrove snake grows to six feet long; although it is equipped with large fangs at the rear of its jaw, it is not considered to be dangerous to man, especially as it is rarely aggressive. It feeds mainly on birds, but sometimes catches and eats bats.

Sometimes called the green whip snake, **The Long-nosed**

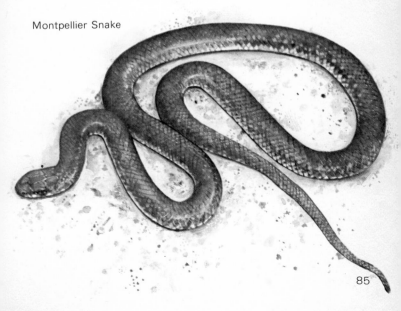

Montpellier Snake

85

The black-and-yellow mangrove snake relies on branches for its support.

Tree Snake *(Dryophis nasutus)* inhabits Ceylon, India, Malaya, and the East Indies. This snake is even thinner and more elongated than many other tree snakes; with its light body it can move fast through bushes and trees. It is normally found in bushes, although it makes occasional forays on the ground. In this species, the difference in size between the sexes is rather pronounced; although females may be as much as six feet long, males are rarely over four foot six inches. Despite the fact that this is a poisonous snake, it is not dangerous to man. It eats lizards, birds, and occasionally other snakes or rodents. Like the boomslang, this snake bites and holds on, refraining from swallowing until the prey is immobilized, which may be as much as half-an-hour after the strike.

The long-nosed tree snake has a most effective threat display when angry. Its scales are green, a useful camouflage against leaves, but the skin between them is black. If the snake inflates itself, it can produce a striking pattern of green on black, adding to the effect by spreading the head and holding the mouth wide open, displaying the black-colored interior.

The long-nosed tree snake is ovoviviparous, producing between 3 and 22 living young at a time.

The Boomslang *(Dispholidus typus)* is found in Africa south of the Sahara, mostly in savanna or open bush country. Like the black-and-yellow mangrove snake this is a mainly arboreal species, although sometimes it comes to the ground to hunt and bask, and it can swim quite well. It moves faster in the trees than on the ground and if frightened it usually makes off in the trees. The boomslang lies perfectly still, in wait for its prey, even though the front of the body may not be supported by branches. It is so good at this and so well camouflaged that it is not unknown for birds to perch on it. This snake has been said to vary in color more than practically any other snake, and it is possible to find adults that are predominantly green, brown, or black with yellow, gray, or green undersides. Even the color of the eyes may vary, being green in some specimens, gray or brown in others. The only constant feature is that brown specimens are nearly always females.

Among the rear-fanged snakes, the boomslang rates as the most serious danger to man. This is not because it is bad-tempered; most specimens are only too pleased to move

Long-nosed Tree Snake

away from a man. If cornered, however, they put on an impressive display, puffing out the neck and foreparts so that the vivid colors of the skin in between the scales are seen. Only if all else fails will a boomslang strike, but if it does the consequences can be serious. The venom gland is not large, but the venom is proportionally stronger than that of many cobras and adders. If the boomslang can get a good grip with its fangs and inject much venom, this can result in death for a man. In its effects, the venom resembles that of adders. How rarely the boomslang uses its ultimate weapon can be judged from the fact that, although it is fairly common, it was for years thought to be more or less harmless. On the average, only about five persons are bitten by boomslangs every ten years. The boomslang prefers to reserve its poison for its prey, chiefly, but not exclusively, tree-dwelling lizards, especially chameleons. The prey is gripped in the jaws until the venom has killed it—about a quarter of an hour for a large chameleon.

The Flying Snake *(Chrysopelea ornata)* is a native of southeast Asia, India and Ceylon. Although only a small snake, rarely more than three feet long, it is one of the most spectacular of all. A flying snake may be one of a whole range of colors, the main background colors usually being black, olive, or green, with markings of yellow, mauve, or red. It is also remarkable for its climbing ability, as it

A boomslang threatening with its neck inflated.

88

Flying snake

can climb smooth perpendicular tree trunks with little trouble. It can also cross gaps of as much as four feet between branches by a type of jumping. The snake coils up, suddenly straightens and launches itself across the gap. Perhaps the most astonishing feat of this snake, however, is that from which it derives its name. The flying snake cannot fly, but it is able to glide remarkably well. To achieve this, it jumps into space and at the same time spreads its ribs and flattens its body, drawing in its under-surface until it is concave. In the way, the snake forms a sort of 'parachute' that slows its fall and allows it to glide a considerable distance. It usually lands in the branches of another tree, resumes its normal cylindrical shape, and goes about its business once again.

The flying snake is a diurnal creature and appears to have no particular food preference, eating whatever it can overpower.

Snail-eating Snake

The Snail-eating Snakes *(Dipsadinae)* —sometimes known as thirst snakes— are a group of about 70 species that form a subfamily of colubrid snakes. They are found in tropical America, in southeastern Asia, and the East Indies. They are all inoffensive and unspectacular snakes that are rarely as much as three feet long. The features that mark them off from other colubrid snakes seem to be largely connected with their specialized diet. The snail-eating snakes are experts at eating mollusks, particularly snails, which they extract from their shells before eating. The snail-eating snakes have a short upper jaw, which bears only four or five small teeth; but the lower jaw is long and can also be swung forward by movement of the skull bone to which it is attached so that it projects in front of the nose. The snake bites a snail at the head; leaving the upper jaw with its teeth firmly embedded, it works the lower jaw up into the shell. The teeth of the lower jaw are then sunk into the prey and the lower jaw is pulled out with a twisting motion that pries out the snail. Apart from the extraordinary development of the lower jaw, which may be three times as long as the upper, the snail-eating snakes also differ from most other snakes in that there is no distensible skin fold in the midline of the lower jaw. Presumably as the prey of the snail-eating snake is so soft and small it never has need to expand its jaws.

The snail-eating snakes are nocturnal and have very large eyes. Many of the more slender ones are arboreal, and egg-laying is the general rule.

Xenodermus (*Xenodermus javanicus*) belongs to a little sub-family of the Colubridae, the Xenoderminae. These snakes live in southeastern Asia and the East Indies, and this species does not possess a common English name. The scales are unusual in that there are no enlarged belly scales and the whole body is therefore covered with fairly small lizard-like scales above and below. The head, too, is covered with small scales and their pattern may be irregular. In many specimens, bare skin is visible between the scales of the body. The scales themselves are bumpy in appearance.

Xenodermus javanicus is a native of the Malayan region and grows to three feet six inches long. It is a lethargic, slow animal and spends much of its time under the surface of wet soil. It is often found in cultivated areas and is mainly a frog-eater. Xeno-dermus is oviparous, but lays only two to four eggs.

Most of the remaining genera within this subfamily are smaller and less well known than *Xenodermus javanicus* and feed on earthworms.

Head of Snail-eating Snake

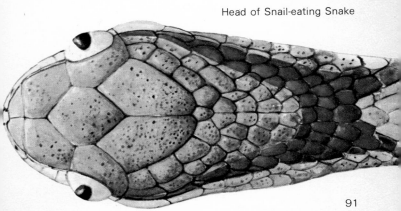

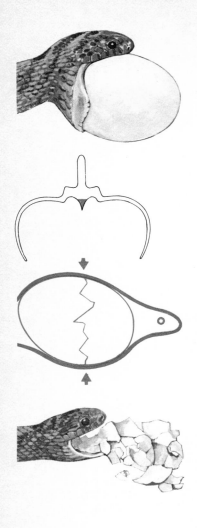

The snake uses its peculiar backbone structure to pierce the egg before rejecting the shell.

The Egg-eating snakes, Dasypeltinae, are another small subfamily of the Colubridae, living mainly in Africa but with one Indian species. The common African egg-eating snake (*Dasypeltis scaber*) grows to about two and a half feet, although some three-foot specimens have been found. The egg-eating snake is remarkable for the way it deals with its food: A three-foot-long snake can comfortably consume a medium-size hen's egg whole. When the snake finds an egg, it flickers its tongue over it, almost infallibly rejecting a rotten one without need to open it. If the egg passes inspection, it is pushed against part of the snake's body, and then the mouth is worked over it until the egg is engulfed; this process may take twenty minutes and leave the snake with its skin stretched paper-thin. The egg moves down until it reaches a constriction in the gullet just behind the projecting vertebrae. Then the snake arches its neck and the egg is held by a sawlike projection of six or eight pointed vertebrae while it is pierced by the pressing of pegs at the back. The egg contents are unable to move toward the head because of a valve arrangement in the gut and are pressed backward toward the stomach. Subsequently the broken shell is regurgitated through the mouth.

The egg-eating snake is largely arboreal, roving widely to detect birds' eggs; it appears to do this, partly at least, by smell. It is itself preyed upon by the boomslang and vine snake, and is quite often killed by man in mistake for the night adder, which it closely resembles in coloration.

When alarmed, the egg-eating snake stridulates by scraping together coils of its body (see illustration below) while puffing itself up with air. It may also make strikes with a wide-open mouth.

The egg-eating snake is oviparous, laying about a dozen eggs; instead of laying them all in one spot, it lays them separately—almost as though it realizes the dangers of being an egg. **The Elephant's Trunk Snake** *(Acrochordus javanicus)*, or Java wart snake, is found in India and throughout southeast Asia as far as New Guinea and the north of Australia. It is most common in Malaya. The elephant's trunk snake has only one close relative, **File Snake,** and the two are placed in a subfamily of their own within the Colubridae, the Acrochordinae (although some specialists prefer to treat them as a separate family). The file snake is about half the size of the elephant's trunk snake and is almost entirely marine, having a flattened tail to assist in swimming.

The elephant's trunk snake grows only to six feet long but may have a girth of a foot. The snake has a very flabby appearance, with much wrinkled loose skin, which accounts for its common name. The elephant's trunk snake is aquatic and nocturnal and can be found in streams and pools, or even at the

The flanks of the egg-eating snake possess strongly keeled scales that stand out when the snake is puffed up and make a sawing noise if rubbed against one another. When alarmed, the snake coils into a disc with the smaller coils near the head and remains in constant motion; adjacent coils move in opposite directions for periods of about 20 seconds.

The fish-eating elephant's trunk snake.

edge of the sea. Its adaptations include nostrils on top of its head that it can close with a flap of cartilage where the nasal passage enters the mouth and small eyes. It is sluggish and may remain motionless for long periods. This snake is a slow but capable swimmer but on land is practically helpless, moving like a huge worm. The scales account partly for this, as both the back and underside are covered with rough scales that may show skin between them. In spite of its unpromising appearance, the skin has considerable use as leather for shoes and handbags; as such, it is known as the skin of 'water snake.' Although normally quiet the elephant's trunk snake can slash sideways and give a nasty bite if provoked.

Another small subfamily of colubrid snakes living in southeast Asia are the Homalopsinae, or fishing snakes. Unlike many snakes, they are able to close their mouths completely with no space left for protrusion of the tongue. The nostrils, like those of the elephant's trunk snake, can be closed, but in this case by a pad on the hind margin of the nostrils that is extended forward. *Homalopsis buccata* is a sluggish snake living in rivers, ponds, or canals, and sometimes burrowing into the mud. It feeds on both fish and frogs. Like other Homalopsine snakes, it is ovovivparous.

Herpeton tentaculatum, from the Indochinese region, grows to three feet long, spending all its life in water. Its native name, 'snake like a board,' is earned from its habit of stiffening so it is rigid when caught. It does not attempt to defend itself in any

File Snake

other way, although it is venomous. *Herpeton* has two rear fangs and venom that can kill fish and frogs, but it is not known whether the venom would be dangerous to humans. This fishing snake possesses two tentacles, scaly appendages on its snout. These are stretched forward and waved under water as lures to tempt fish close to the snake's head. When the fish is in range, the snake strikes at it and kills it.

Herpeton tentaculatum displaying its tentacles to lure fish.

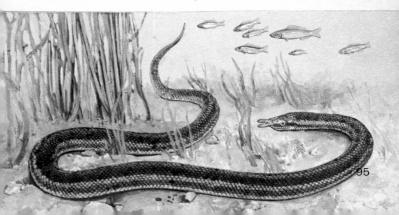

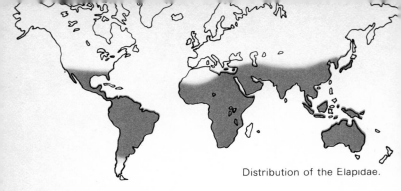

THE ELAPIDAE

The family Elapidae is found throughout the warm regions of both the Old and the New World. In most places where they occur, the elapids are in a minority among the snakes; in one continent, Australia, the majority of snakes are elapids. In Australia, nine out of every ten species of snakes belong to the cobra family.

The elapids are all proteroglyph snakes—that is, they have the poison fangs at the front end of the upper jaw, on the maxilla. The fangs are carried rigid in the jaw and are therefore always erect and ready to be used in biting. The venom gland discharges into the top of the fang and poison then runs down a tube in the tooth into the wound. In some specimens, there is a slight flow of venom all the time. Although the cobra fang normally possesses a tubular structure, a small groove can be seen at the front of the tooth. This probably represents the place where folds from either side of the venom groove have met, showing how the cobra fang may well have developed from the open-groove type of fang. Cobra venom is usually neurotoxic (see p. 150). Most of the elapids are oviparous, except the Australian species; a small number of species have developed parental care as far as guarding the nest or eggs.

Cobras are well known for their characteristic wide neck-hood, but this is well developed in only a few elapids. Those cobras that possess a hood do not display it all the time; it serves as a threat display when the cobra is frightened or annoyed, apparently having evolved to scare off predators.

In the neck region, the cobra has long and movable ribs; it is these, combined with inflation with air from the lungs, that provide the distension for the skin of the neck. Some species have spectacle or eye-markings on the hood to enhance the frightening appearance.

Cobras

The Indian Cobra *(Naja naja)* is found over southern Asia from Iran, south through India to Ceylon, and eastward to southeast Asia, the Malay Archipelago, and even the Philippine Islands. As is often the case with wide-ranging snakes, several sub-species can be distinguished. The specimens from West Pakistan, India, and Ceylon are normally those that show the spectacle marking on the hood, for which this cobra is famous. Specimens from Assam and regions to the east often have a single ring marking in place of the double spectacles; those snakes from the west of the Indian cobra's range have the spectacle replaced by several black bars.

The Indian cobra is not a very large snake, the average adult growing to between four and five feet long. Only a few individuals grow to seven feet. The Indian cobra preys largely on rats, which often live near human dwellings, and this helps to make this snake a danger to human life. It also eats mice, frogs, birds, and eggs.

The Indian cobra may be found in practically any type of country, forested or open, even where there is a large human population; in dry places, or in the dry seasons, it is rarely far from water. In the daytime, when its eyesight appears poor, the Indian cobra will usually move away quickly if disturbed. At night, however, the snake is more inclined to be aggressive and, as it sees well in dim light, it is able

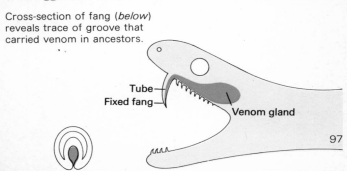

Cross-section of fang (*below*) reveals trace of groove that carried venom in ancestors.

Tube
Fixed fang
Venom gland

to strike accurately. Early evening is the time when the Indian cobra does most of its hunting, and this is when, in inhabited regions, it is most likely to bite a man. Because many of the natives of India and southeast Asia habitually walk around with bare legs, they are especially liable to be bitten by snakes: it has been estimated that cobras bite approximately 10,000 people a year in India. Because of the large number of people bitten by Indian cobras, the venom is probably the most studied in the world, although even with cobra venom only one in ten bites are fatal.

When annoyed, the Indian cobra raises about one-third of its body and spreads its hood, which is the best developed of all the cobras. A few Indian cobras have developed the additional defense of spitting venom for a short distance.

Illustration of cobra neck ribs.

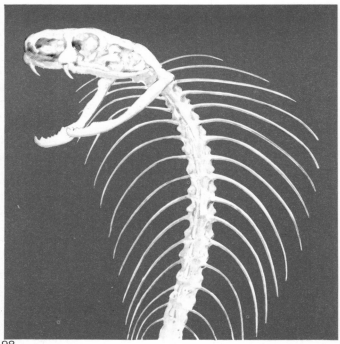

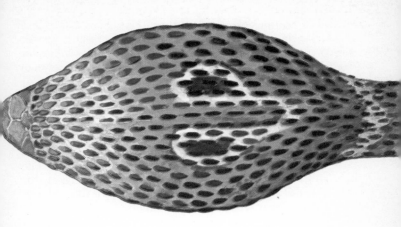

Cobra neck inflated showing eye-markings.

Indian cobras mate at the beginning of the year, and 10 to 24 eggs are laid in a rough nest in May. The parents may stay together until the young hatch and usually remain near the nest to act as guards. When the young hatch, they are slightly less than a foot long. Baby cobras are more aggressive than their parents and are able to rear up, spread hoods, and strike, while still emerging from the egg.

When cobras strike, they do so simply by falling forward and so they must be close to their victim when they attempt it. When a man is struck, it is invariably below the knee; because of this, a large measure of protection can be obtained simply by wearing high boots.

The King Cobra *(Ophiophagus hannah),* or hamadryad, is now usually assigned to its own genus. It is the giant among the cobra family and is the largest of the poisonous snakes. A grown adult can be 14 feet long or more; the record is held by a specimen 18 feet 4 inches long. The king cobra is found in India, southern China, and over most of southeast Asia, but it is not a common snake. It is chiefly an animal of the plains, although in peninsular India its range corresponds with the mountains and hills. Unlike the Indian cobra, it does much of its hunting in the daytime, and it may be found on the ground, in the water, or in trees, where it is a good climber. The king cobra is almost entirely a snake-eater (and thus its genus name, *Ophiphagus,* which means 'snake-eater'). It will eat snakes of all kinds, harmless or poisonous, including pythons and cobras; in some cases it has been known to turn cannibal and eat smaller members of its own species.

The king cobra is one of the most aggressive of all snakes and it may attack without provocation, especially close to its nest; but it is unpredictable and may just as easily move away from disturbance. Certainly a large king cobra is a force to be reckoned with, because it may be able to raise its head five to six feet from the gound before it strikes. The king cobra may be one of the most intelligent snakes, for it quickly learns not to strike at a glass cage front in captivity; it also shows fairly well-developed parental behavior.

The king cobra mates in January and builds its nest in April or May; it is the only cobra that habitually makes its own nest. It lays twenty to forty eggs and guards them until they hatch. The parents usually remain together until the eggs are hatched, the female remaining in the upper chamber

A king cobra's size
compared to that of
an average man.

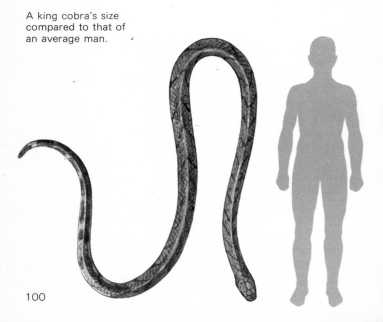

Egyptian Cobra

of the nest and the male either there or on guard outside. Hatchling king cobras are about 20 inches long, already a respectable size for a poisonous snake.

The Egyptian Cobra *(Naja haje)* is found in Africa from Morocco to Arabia and southward as far as Zambia and southwest Africa, living mostly in arid country. Its chief prey are toads, although birds are captured when possible; the venom of the Egyptian cobra seems extemely fast-acting on the latter. The Egyptian cobra grows up to eight feet six inches long, larger than the Indian cobra; but it is not capable of spreading its hood out to such an extent, as is the case with all the African cobras.

In spite of its size, and the large amount of venom it secretes, the Egyptian cobra is not troublesome to humans and few fatalities have been known. One of the more famous fatalities may have been Cleopatra, who is reputed to have taken her own life with an asp. The name asp is sometimes given to the Egyptian cobra, and it is probable that the snake in question was a cobra as death from cobra bites is much less painful than from bites of those adders known as asps.

The Black-and-White Cobra *(Naja melanoleuca)*, also known as the black-lipped cobra and forest cobra, lives in Africa from Gambia in the west to Kenya in the east and southward as far as Malawi and Angola. It averages about five feet long, when adult, but specimens eight and a half feet long have been known. This snake prefers a damp environment and not too

Black-and-white cobra (*left*) and black-necked cobra (*below*).

much heat and is nearly always encountered in humid forest areas, either on land or in water. Often a black-and-white cobra will have a lair in a hollow tree or old termites' nest and will go back there at great speed if it is frightened. Normally this snake is not aggressive toward man, and eats fish and frogs and also small mammals and reptiles.

The Black-necked Cobra *(Naja nigricollis),* or spitting cobra, is found over wide areas of Africa south of the Sahara, its range roughly corresponding with that of the black-and-white cobra, except that the black-necked is a savanna rather than a forest creature. It is a small snake, growing usually to three or four feet; no specimen longer than seven feet four inches is known. The black-necked cobra is nocturnal and preys on rodents and reptiles that it hunts on the ground, although it will climb trees to reach birds' eggs. It may make its home in an abandoned termites' nest or among rotting logs. It is not aggressive and the younger specimens may sham death if molested. The venom is, however, quite potent and to protect itself this snake may, like the ringhals, spit its venom for several feet.

The Ringhals (*Hemachatus hemachatus*) lives in the south of Africa from the Cape as far north as Rhodesia. Most adults are only just over three feet, but some specimens nearly double that length have been found. Rodents, frogs, and birds' eggs are eaten. It has a strongly neurotoxic venom but usually shows a reluctance to bite as it has other ways of dealing with an aggressor. One of these is simply to feign death, turning the head and front of the body upside-down and letting the mouth hang open. If it is touched in this position, however, it may well bite. The other form of defense is to spray its venom. The poison duct down the fang of a ringhals turns outward at the end. If a ringhals is annoyed, it rears up in typical cobra fashion, opens its mouth, and pulls back the lower jaw so that the fangs are exposed. If the aggressor persists, venom is ejected through the fangs by muscular pressure on the poison glands and is sprayed for a distance of six to eight feet. The ringhals leans back slightly and aims at the eye region. Normally venom that hits the eyes cannot reach the bloodstream in sufficient quantities to be fatal; but it may have a very unpleasant action on the eye membranes causing pain and, in severe cases, permanent blindness. In zoos where the ringhals is kept, it is usual for keepers to wear goggles when tending them.

A ringhals spitting venom, with diagram showing how venom can be aimed from the fang.

The Black Mamba *(Dendroaspis polylepis)* is the largest African poisonous snake and is found over much of the continent south of the Sahara. An average-sized adult is some nine or ten feet long, but some grow to 14 feet. In spite of their name, black mambas are never actually black but are dark brown to various shades of gray. They are not normally found in forest regions, although as well as being quick and alert on the ground, they are also good climbers and can easily scale bushes. Often a black mamba will have its home among rocks or in a hole excavated by a rodent, and it will rarely stray far from water. It finds most of its food in bushes and trees, mainly eating squirrels and birds.

Although it will often take off when disturbed, the black mamba has a reputation for being ferocious. For a snake, it is comparatively fast moving; as it strikes quickly and has potent venom, it is a dangerous adversary. The fangs of the mamba are quite large and situated at the front of the long jaw, with a gap between them and the other teeth. They do not possess a hood like the true cobras but may inflate their necks when angry.

Found in Africa, with much the same distribution as the black mamba, and living mainly in savanna country, the **Green Mamba** *(Dendroaspis angusticeps)* is a distinct species. It is considerably smaller than the black mamba— usually about five feet long, with a maximum of nine—and is, if anything, more arboreal. The green mamba has a prehensile tail, which it uses when climbing in the leafy thickets that are its chosen haunts. Its vivid green color is extremely

Black Mamba

Green Mamba

difficult to detect against such a background. Between the scales, the skin is black in color; the combination of black and green, when an annoyed snake inflates itself, produces a very effective display.

In the trees, the green mamba stalks the birds and lizards that are its food, seizing them with the fangs of the upper jaw and also with enlarged teeth in the lower jaw that lie beneath the fangs. The teeth in the lower jaw, of course, contain no poison ducts.

The green mamba is much less aggressive than the black mamba and usually flees rather than stand its ground, but it can give a dangerous bite. Sometimes it is confused with the boomslang, but the latter has much bigger eyes, shorter head, and rough scales, as well as the fangs in a different position.

The Death Adder *(Acanthophis antarcticus)* is not a true adder at all; like all the other venomous Australian snakes, it is a member of the cobra family, the Elapidae. In the shape of its body and head, however, it is viper-like, being three feet long with a wide body, flattened head, and short tail with a spiked tip. Like many of the true adders, it is lethargic and instead of moving away from a disturbance sits tight, relying on its camouflage. The death adder lives throughout Australia, except in the central desert, and may be black, fawn, gray, or reddish, normally corresponding with the color of the soil of its home. When this snake is annoyed, it flattens its body. If stepped on, this small snake can give a serious bite, and about half the bites are fatal. Some Australians believe it stings with the tail, but this is not so.

Death Adder

The death adder feeds mostly on lizards but may strike at anything it can reach with great speed. The tail is like a segmented spike and this snake often lies waving the tail, just in front of the head, as a lure to attract lizards. The death adder bears about twelve young at a time.

The Kraits are a small group of about a dozen species living in southern Asia, usually in open plains country. These elapid snakes are shy and inoffensive, and rarely bite a man unless severely provoked; normal action for a krait when caught is to coil and hide its head. The scales of kraits are shiny and have a polished appearance. A peculiarity of this snake is that the iris of the eye is colorless and the eye appears to have a very large pupil, probably an adaptation

A banded krait chasing another snake.

to the krait's nocturnal way of life. Kraits feed mostly on other snakes, both venomous and harmless, but eat other animals as well.

The Banded Krait *(Bungarus fasciatus)* can be found in Assam and southeast Asia and is very rarely over six feet in length. The Siamese name for this snake is the 'triangular snake' because of its high backbone ridge. The banded krait is slow-moving and has never been known to bite humans. In fact, many of the natives of its homelands believe that it is not poisonous.

The Common Krait *(Bungarus caeruleus)* lives in India and West Pakistan. (A related species, *B. ceylonicus,* lives in Ceylon.) It is under five feet in length. It lays eggs in April and the ten-inch-long young hatch from the end of May onward, growing at the rate of about a foot in each of their first three years. The common krait has exceedingly strong venom, four times as potent as that of the Indian cobra; but as it rarely bites humans, it can be considered relatively harmless.

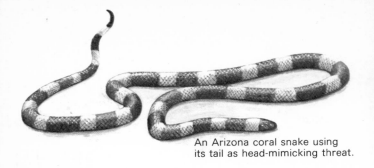

An Arizona coral snake using
its tail as head-mimicking threat.

Coral Snakes

In Asia, Africa, and Australia live elapid snakes that have burrowing habits and bright coloration and are called 'coral snakes.' The true coral snakes, however, number about 40 species and live in the New World, mostly in South and Central America. All have bodies with bands of contrasting colors—red, black, and yellow, although some have only red and black bands, while others have white instead of yellow. The purpose of this coloration is not really understood. It is remarkable that these secretive and often burrowing snakes should be so highly colored since they are visible for a comparatively short time. Perhaps the surprise element helps in using these colors as a warning. When in danger, most of the coral snakes make use of their tails in a head-mimicking threat.

Some harmless American snakes have a very similar color to the coral snakes, notably the scarlet king snake, sometimes called false coral snake. The scarlet king snake differs from any North American coral snake in that the rings continue across the lower surface and there are black rings between any red or yellow bands; in the North American coral snakes, the red and yellow rings are in contact. The snouts are also different colors. Nevertheless, the harmless and venomous 'coral' snakes are sufficiently similar to be confused without careful examination. It may be that the harmless snakes derive a certain amount of protection from this coincidence, as well as equipping themselves for camouflage.

Like the other elapids, the coral snakes are front-fanged and venomous. The venom of some, at least, would appear to be highly neurotoxic, but the fangs are small and are rarely

Common Coral Snake

Wied's Coral Snake *(right)*

used to bite humans. Coral snakes can usually be handled without biting, but to do so with bare hands is certainly risky: of the few bites that have been delivered to humans by coral snakes, a high percentage have been fatal.

The Common Coral Snake *(Micrurus fulvius)* is found from Florida north to the Carolinas and west to Texas and Mexico. It is also called the Harlequin Coral Snake. It grows to a maximum of 47 inches, although the average specimen is slightly over two feet long. It is quite a common snake but rarely seen, generally emerging only at night. Most of the time is spent underground or under logs, stones, or dense undergrowth. The main food of the common coral snake is other snakes and lizards. As in the cobras, there is only a single tooth, the poison fang, on the maxillary bone.

The Wied's Coral Snake *(Micrurus corallus)* lives in the tropical regions of South America, and grows to a maximum length of two and a half feet.

The Arizona Coral Snake *(Micruroides euryxanthus)* lives in Arizona and northwestern Mexico. It has one or two teeth on the maxillary in addition to the fang. This snake grows to only 20 inches long and feeds on other snakes.

Australian Snakes

The Tiger Snake *(Notechis scutatus)* lives in eastern and southern Australia, getting its name from its most common color variety of gray-brown with yellow stripes. It is not always obviously striped and may be many colors from yellow or orange to olive, brown, or black. In southern Australia it is a common snake; since its venom is extremely potent, the chances of getting a bad bite from one are considerably high. It is relatively stout and generally about four feet long, although eight foot specimens are known. It is generally encountered in swamps, where it may be found climbing in bushes or on the ground. The tiger snake produces large numbers of young, up to fifty in a litter; like most of the Australian elapids, it is ovoviviparous.

The Australian Brown Snake *(Demansia textilis)* lives in the eastern parts of New South Wales and Queensland and East New Guinea; it is usually found in the more arid areas with sandy soil. The brown snake is usually five feet in length when adult, but exceptional specimens may be seven feet. These small-headed snakes are fast-moving and irascible, and it takes little to annoy them. If they get the chance, these snakes will strike again and again. In a striking position, they are

Tiger snake with a typical litter of many young.

Adult Australian brown snake from the bush *(above)* and adult from the desert *(below)*.

a little like the true cobras because they rear up, throwing their neck into an S-shape and flattening it slightly before lunging down in their strike.

The brown snake is the only one among the Australian elapids to produce eggs rather than living young. When the young hatch, they are striped, usually sepia or light brown, and they retain this color for over a year. As they become adult their color changes, largely seeming to correspond with their habitat; those living in the bush become a plain olive, and those in very dry desert areas become a plain tan.

The Australian black snake rarely bites and its venom is not very strong.

The Australian Black Snake *(Pseudechis porphyriacus)* is found in eastern and southern Australia, in the damp mountain forests or swamps, where it catches frogs, lizards, and a few small birds and mammals for food. It may also occasionally turn cannibal. When annoyed, it spreads its neck in a similar fashion to a cobra, but the hood is poorly developed.

The Taipan *(Oxyuranus scutellatus)* is perhaps the most deadly and ferocious of the Australian snakes, if not of all snakes everywhere. At the same time, it is probably one of the least dangerous as it lives in the northeast well away from any large centers of population, and rarely comes in contact with man. If a man is bitten by this monster, there is little hope of recovery; death within a few minutes is the most likely result.

The taipan is ten feet long with venom second only to the tiger snake in strength.

When angered, the Australian copperhead may rear up.

The Australian Copperhead (*Denisonia superba*) lives in southeast Australia and Tasmania; as it lives near centers of population, it is more likely to be a danger than the taipan, although in general it is shy. It grows to five feet long and perhaps a little larger in Tasmania; its diet is lizards and frogs. The Australian copperhead is hardy, emerging from hibernation before most other snakes and retreating later for the winter. It is of special interest because it is one of the few snakes with a primitive placenta.

The Bandy-Bandy (*Vermicella annulata*) grows to a maximum of two and a half feet. It looks much like some of the burrowing snakes, but rarely burrows except in ready-made holes. The bandy-bandy is widely believed to be dangerous; but although technically venomous, it does not seem to do much harm to man.

The bandy-bandy is more liable to coil up rather than to bite.

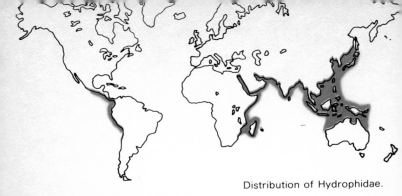

Distribution of Hydrophidae.

THE HYDROPHIDAE

The Seasnakes *(Hydrophidae)* form a small family of about 50 species, closely allied to the cobras. They live in the warm seas near the coast of Asia extending from the Persian Gulf as far as Japan and near the Australian coast and some of the oceanic islands. The widest-ranging species has also crossed the Pacific and specimens can be seen off the western coast of northern South America. The whole family is marine but the species within the family show a variety of adaptation ranging from those that can still move on land, to those that are completely independent of land and are helpless when placed on it. Most of the seasnakes have lost the large belly-shields found in ordinary snakes and so cannot get a proper grip on land. Most of the seasnakes, too, have valves in their nostrils to exclude water and can draw the front of their windpipe up to where the nostrils open to the mouth — both valuable adaptations for an aquatic animal that still breathes air but may have its head partly submerged when doing so. The lung is very large and stretches practically the complete length of the snake, although the rear part seems to act as a kind of float, rather than to take in oxygen, and may also store air for use in dives.

The seasnakes have their bodies flattened from side to side to a variable extent. But all of them have their tail flattened into the form of a paddle to drive them through the water. Seasnakes swim, as do other snakes, by throwing their body into longitudinal waves running from the head to the tail.

None of the seasnakes are exceptionally large in size, and it seems very unlikely that these true serpents of the sea gave rise to the fables of the 'Great Sea Serpent.' Sighting of giant squids far more probably gave rise to a belief in this mythical monster.

The longest species of seasnake grows only to eight feet, and most of the species are between four and five feet long. In spite of their aquatic adaptation, most seasnakes favor shallow seas not far from land, especially if the waters are somewhat sheltered; they are often found in the waters outside estuaries. Little is known of their feeding habits but they are, as far as is known, entirely fish-eating animals — with a particular preference for eels, presumably because these fish are an easy shape for a snake to swallow. It is sometimes possible to get a seasnake to take bait from a fishing line.

The seasnakes kill their prey with venom; like the cobras, seasnakes are rigid front-fanged snakes. Tests have shown that most seasnakes have very strong venom; among their number they include the snakes with the most potent venom of all, stronger even than the cobras or tiger snakes. If an eel is bitten, it stiffens and dies within seconds. Yet all the

Banded Laticauda

seasnakes seem most reluctant to use their venom and, even in those places where they are common, they never attack people swimming in the water. They are often caught in nets along with fish and are unraveled from the net and thrown out by the fishermen barehanded. The men usually suffer no harm, as only when handled really roughly, or severely provoked, will the seasnake bite a man. In some places, the seasnakes are made use of as food; they can be caught very easily after dark as they are attracted by lamps.

Seasnakes appear to be active both at night and during the day. Early in the day, before the sun becomes too powerful, and sometimes in the late afternoon, they can be seen in large numbers up at the surface presumbly basking in the sun. If disturbed, they dive below the surface.

One or two observers have reported seeing seasnakes in huge numbers on a single day. One report in particular (by a Mr. Lowe writing in 1932) described passing in a steamer off the island of Sumatra when a solid mass of sea-snakes were squirming and twisting together over an area ten feet wide and 60 miles long. Such an aggregation must have held literally millions of seasnakes—in this case, the

A *Microcephalophis gracilis* catching an eel.

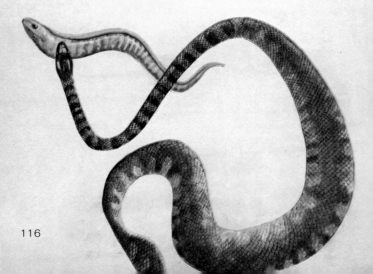

Black-and-Yellow Seasnake

species *Astrotia stokesi,* a seasnake growing up to six feet long but with a massive girth and colored red and black. The significance of this unforgettable sight is not known, but it seems likely that this was the mating time for these snakes.

Found from Japan to Australia and the Bay of Bengal, **the Banded Laticauda** *(Laticauda laticaudata)* grows to some three and a half feet in length. The genus *Laticauda* is still tied to the land, as these snakes are egg-laying; they spend much of their time out of water, never venturing to the deep ocean. *Laticauda* still has the wide ventral scales typical of land snakes and, although it does not move fast on land, it is not particularly awkward.

Microcephalophis gracilis is a seasnake about three feet long with the peculiarity that the abdomen has a diameter about four times that of the head and neck. *Microcephalophis* is a specialized eel-eater, and its shape may help it in some way to catch its chosen food.

Of all the seasnakes, **the Black-and-Yellow Seasnake** *(Pelamis platurus)* is perhaps the most highly adapted for life in the sea, for it is much flattened from side to side and is a fast swimmer. Unlike the other seasnakes, it is sometimes ecountered hundreds of miles from land, and is the only one which has crossed to the eastern side of the Pacific Ocean. This snake grows up to three and a half feet long and does not have enlarged belly scales. Like most seasnakes, it gives birth to live young and has no need at all to come to land.

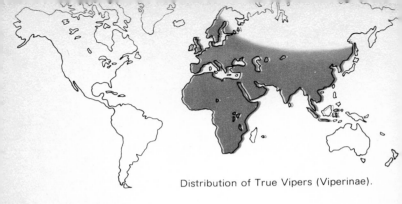

Distribution of True Vipers (Viperinae).

THE VIPERIDAE

The vipers are present in all parts of the world where snakes occur except Madagascar and the Australasian region. It is perhaps not surprising that the vipers are absent from these islands; these areas have been cut off from the main land masses of the world for an extremely long time, besides which the vipers are in many ways the most highly evolved snakes and probably one of the latest groups to evolve.

The vipers are the snakes in which the poison apparatus has developed to its greatest extent. The large venom glands—partly accounting for the great width of head—are connected by ducts to two very large fangs. These have channels down their centers forming an excellent hypodermic injection system. Unlike the cobras, no trace of this channel appears on the surface of the fang. The fangs of most vipers are so long that it would be impossible to shut the mouth if it were not for the fact that the vipers have evolved with a folding-away device. When at rest, the fangs lie directed backward along the upper jaw; if the snake is about to bite, muscular action rotates the maxillary bone on which the fang is situated and erects the fang ready for use.

The habits of the viper family are what might be expected from their physique and venom equipment. Most are terrestrial, although a few have taken to the trees, employing a prehensile tail. There are no aquatic vipers and many species

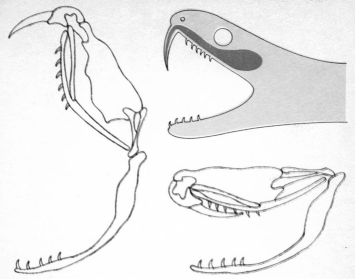

The folding fangs and venom provide the vipers with the most formidable weaponry of any group of snakes.

avoid water; a small group only, the mole vipers, have taken to burrowing. Most vipers lie in wait for their food on the ground, until a small animal is within striking distance; they then make a swift jab with their fangs. Vipers rarely hold on to their prey, but remove the fangs after the initial lunge, which injects sufficient venom for the purpose. Vipers never chase their food and may allow the bitten victim to move away; a few minutes after, when the venom has done its fatal work, the viper trails its prey, finds it, and consumes it.

Perhaps the most dangerous trait of the vipers is their habit of relying on their camouflage to conceal, instead of moving away when disturbed, with the result that they may be inadvertently stepped on. A general characteristic of the viper is that the shields on the head have been replaced by small scales.

In the viper family, Viperidae, there are two divisions, or sub-families: the Viperinae, which includes the true vipers; and the Crotalinae, which includes the rattlesnakes and their allies. The Viperinae are found mostly in Africa, where

119

there is the greatest variety of species, and also in Europe and in Asia; only a few species are found in the southern regions of Asia. They differ from the Crotalinae in that they lack a facial pit.

Vipers

The Common European Viper, or Adder *(Vipera berus)* is the most northerly ranging of all snakes. In Britain it is the only snake in Scotland; in Scandinavia, it is found as far north as 68° N., just within the Arctic circle. The adder—as it is commonly known in England—is found from Britain right across Europe, except in the extreme south, and across Asia to China and eastern Russia. It is one of the most widespread of all snakes.

Individual European vipers show much variability in their colors and markings but nearly always there is a dark V- or X-shaped mark behind the head and a dark zigzag line down the back.

This viper may be found in almost any kind of habitat but it prefers dry sandy heathlands. It is mainly active during the day, but it may also kill prey after dark, eating a wide range of food, principally common lizards and voles.

Although this snake is hardy and may emerge from hibernation in February or March, it is not until April that the snakes mate. Some male vipers appear to hold a 'territory' that they defend against others, and rivalry of two or three males for a single female is common. Rivalries are resolved by a ritualized fight in which the males rear up and try and press one another to the ground. The weaker gives way and, although the victor may chase the loser, he does not bite. The males court the females by running the tongue and chin along their backs. After mating, the females ovulate and the fertilized eggs undergo a four or five month development period before 6 to 20 young are born at the beginning of September.

European vipers do not normally present a danger to humans unless trodden on, provoked, or foolishly handled; death from the bite of this snake is most uncommon.

The shape of an adder is such that if it is picked up by the tail its muscles are unable to lift its head to deliver a bite on the hand holding it. However, handling vipers in this way

Common European Viper

is a job best left to the expert. There is no reason to kill such snakes when they are seen because they represent no real risk to humans and may in fact be beneficial in helping to keep down rodents. These snakes are difficult to keep in captivity as they often refuse to feed.

Sand Viper

The Sand Viper *(Vipera ammodytes)* — sometimes known as the long-nosed or nose-horned viper — can be found in the Balkan peninsula, northern Italy, and southern Austria. The sand viper has a slightly greater maximum size than the common European viper and a few specimens reach three feet long. A distinctive feature is the presence of a small horn covered with little scales on the snout.

The sand viper is a lethargic animal and most of its movements are slow. It is found in dry country and, like the common viper, it is fond of basking in the sun.

Despite the fact that the sand viper is of peaceable disposition, it possesses the most formidable venom apparatus of any European snake. The fangs may be half an inch long, and the venom is the strongest among European vipers. With these weapons, the sand viper preys on mice and voles; even small rats and sometimes a bird or lizard is taken. Sand vipers are ovoviviparous; the young feed on small lizards and baby mice before progressing to adult diet.

The venom of the sand viper is used to produce antivenin for the bite of European vipers and the snake is farmed for this purpose. The sand viper tolerates captivity much better than the common viper, thriving in almost any kind of surroundings and usually taking food easily from the start.

The Asp Viper *(Vipera aspis)* lives in Europe from the Balkans across Italy and Germany to France. It grows to just over two feet long, and the males may be larger than the females.

The asp viper often lies almost buried in soft soil or sand, wriggling from side to side and getting down into the ground so that only the eyes and nose are visible. It is able to move by sidewinding if it needs to. It may be active either in the day or at night, feeding on lizards and small birds and mammals. Young asp vipers eat worms and insect food.

The asp viper mates in April or May; about ten young are born three months later, each about seven inches long. Specimens have occasionally been found that may have been hybrids between the asp viper and the common European viper.

Asp Viper

Russell's Viper *(Vipera russelli)* is one of the relatively small number of the Viperinae found in southern Asia. It occurs in India, where it is the common viper, and also down into southeast Asia, including the East Indian archipelago. It is often known by its native names of 'Daboia' or 'Tic-polonga.' In some parts of its range this snake is exceedingly common but it is scarce in others. It is a large snake, growing to five and a half feet in length, but is much more slenderly built than are most vipers.

Its food consists principally of rodents but it will consume frogs and lizards too. Russell's viper is ovoviviparous and may have between 20 and 60 young at a time.

Because of the large amount of venom it can inject at one time, the Russell's viper is a particularly dangerous snake. As well as typical viper hematoxic poison (see page 150), the venom contains a large amount of nerve poison, and for this reason can be fast acting as well as extremely unpleasant. In the regions where it lives, the Russell's viper is one of the most dreaded of all snakes.

The Horned Asp *(Cerastes cerastes)* is found in North Africa and Arabia and is especially common in Egypt. It is a small snake, rarely exceeding two feet in length, but the body is comparatively wide and the tail very short. The

Russell's Viper

horned asp lives in desert regions, and much of its movement over the shifting sands is accomplished by sidewinding. The eyes are directed upward so that the snake can see when almost completely buried. Most individuals of this species have over each eye a sharp pointed hornlike scale; this probably serves to protect the eye from sun and sand but is also a greatly prized characteristic of these snakes for the snake-charmers of Egypt. For some reason, a horned viper is better thought of than those specimens lacking this embellishment; if Egyptian snake-charmers capture a hornless individual, they may remedy the deficiency by driving a spine from another animal, usually a hedgehog, through the upper jaw to emerge above the eye. A good many of the vipers mutilated in this way apparently survive for long periods and, on occasion, have been offered to zoo snake-collectors as 'horned asps.'

The keels of the scales on the side of the horned asp are so arranged that, if the snake wriggles its body, the keels throw sand upward and allow the snake to sink below the surface of the ground and so remain hidden.

Horned Asp

125

Saw-scaled Viper

The Saw-scaled Viper *(Echis carinatus)* can be found in Ceylon, peninsular India, and westward to equatorial Africa. The saw-scaled viper lives in dry country and seems to be able to endure the heat of direct sun much better than most desert snakes. It only grows to between 20 inches and two and a half feet in length, but it can be dangerous as its habit is to lie in sand with only the head exposed. It is a nervous snake, quick to strike, with the ability to fling itself a foot or more in the air to deliver a bite. The venom of this snake is highly toxic, and the bite of the saw-scaled viper is often fatal.

If it is disturbed, the saw-scaled viper inflates its body, so that the saw-toothed keels on the scales at the sides of the body stick out; it then throws its body into loops scraping one against another and producing a noise like a violent bubbling. **The Puff Adder** *(Bitis arietans)* occurs all over Africa, except on the northern coast; it is also found in Arabia. It may be found in almost any kind of country except tropical rain forests but is most often found in dry savanna or semi-desert.

The puff adder grows up to five feet long, but is very thick-bodied and may be nine inches in girth. A large specimen may have fangs an inch long.

During the day, the puff adder usually hides under sand or in grass, emerging at night to hunt rodents. It lies in wait on a trail used by these animals; when one approaches, the snake strikes swiftly, then pulls back and waits. The venom is potent and may kill a rat within seconds; the puff adder may use its long fangs to hook food into its mouth. Sometimes it feeds on cold-blooded prey such as frogs, which may be swallowed without the use of venom.

Because of its sluggish nature and camouflage, the puff adder is dangerous and probably accounts for more cases of snakebite in Africa than any other snake. It can, moreover, strike forward or sideways like lightning, although fatal bites may not cause death for 24 hours.

The puff adder is ovoviviparous. It mates in November or December; about five months later, a litter of young are produced, which may be as many as 70 although 20 to 40 is more usual. The snake gets its name from its habit of inflating itself and hissing in and out violently when it is alarmed.

Puff Adder

Night Adder

The Night Adder *(Causus rhombeatus)* is found in Africa south of the Sahara; it grows to about two feet long. It is, in some ways, one of the least typical of the viper family, because it has a slender build and has a longer tapering tail than is usual in a viper. Instead of the many little scales covering the surface of the head, the night adder has large head-shields like a colubrid snake, and this is probably a sign that this is rather a primitive viper. The breeding habits are odd, too, because, unlike the majority of vipers, the night adder lays eggs. It is also less sluggish than most vipers. All in all, it is a peculiar viper; but like all the members of the family it has folding fangs although they are rather small. The night adder is highly specialized in the development of its venom glands, for these are not just situated in the upper jaw but lie in the neck region extending on each side of the backbone for a length of up to four inches. A long duct connects glands to fangs. In spite of the enormous development of venom glands, the night adder is not quick to use its venom even against its normal prey, frogs and toads. Often these animals are simply seized and swallowed, although the venom would kill them quickly.

As their name suggests, night adders are mostly active at night, but may bask in the daytime. They live on the ground, often near water, and may make their home in a pile of vegetation. In the summer, they lay about a dozen eggs.

The Gaboon Viper *(Bitis gabonica)* lives in Africa south of the Sahara. It is a creature of the tropical rain forests, but like the puff adder has eyes directed upward and nostrils on the top of the snout—adaptations for lying buried. The Gaboon viper reaches a length of five and a half feet but is very thick-bodied; one specimen had a girth of over fourteen inches and weighed 18 pounds. The fangs of the largest specimens may be two inches long, and the venom is probably the most potent of all the vipers; in spite of this, the Gaboon viper is normally very docile. If it is annoyed, this snake behaves like the puff adder, flattening its body, hissing loudly, and making lunges at its adversary.

The Gaboon viper is active at night, hunting small ground-living birds and mammals. Like many vipers, the strike is fast; occasionally the Gaboon viper does not withdraw after its strike but may hold on until its prey is dead. The fangs are not used as hooks as in the puff adder.

Gaboon Viper

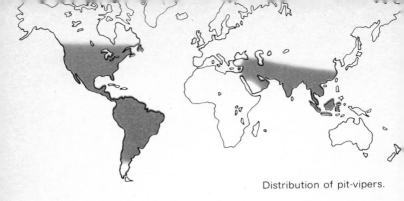

Distribution of pit-vipers.

Pit-Vipers

Most of the Crotalinae, or pit-vipers, live in the New World, but some snakes of this sub-family live in eastern Asia. The feature that distinguishes the pit-vipers from other members of the family is the possession of two facial pits that function as specialized sense organs. For a long time, there was doubt among zoologists as to what these pits actually did; it is now known that they are heat detectors. The facial pits are situated on the snout of the snake between the eyes and the nostrils, usually lower on the cheek than either of these. In some cases, it is easy to mistake a pit for a nostril at a casual glance, but the nostrils of pit-vipers are always at the tip of the snout.

The pit is really a double structure. There is one large cavity at the front with the opening onto the snout; behind this there is a smaller cavity with a tiny opening to the air, just visible in front of the eye. Between these two cavities is a thin membrane well supplied with nerves that are very sensitive to warmth and able to detect small differences in temperature between the air in the front cavity and that in the back. In other words, the snake is able to sense warm objects lying in front of the pit. As the snake has a facial pit on each side of its snout and the fields covered by the two pits overlap, the snake can have a 'stereoscopic' heat sense that enables it to judge distances accurately. It has been shown that rattlesnakes can respond to warm objects that produce a difference of temperature of only one-third of a degree Farenheit at the membrane. A human hand can be detected at more than a foot range. Using their heat-sensitive pits, blindfolded rattlesnakes can strike accurately at prey. These pits are obviously a useful device for a cold-blooded animal seeking warm-blooded prey; they would be useless to an animal seeking prey at about the same temperature as itself. A pit-viper, hunting at night, would be especially helped by its facial pits.

The American Copperhead (*Agkistrodon contortrix*) is found in the eastern United States from Florida to Texas in the south and north to New England. The length of an adult specimen is usually about two and a half feet long; the largest measured was four foot five inches in length. In some places, they are very common; however, they are usually found in areas with plenty of cover.

They catch and eat whatever is available including insects such as caterpillars and cicadas, rather unimposing fare for a poisonous snake of this size, although the diet includes mice and shrews.

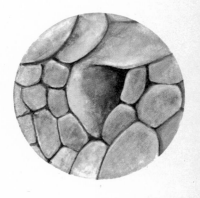

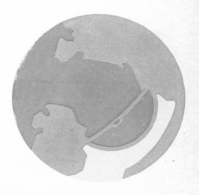

Views of the heat-sensitive facial pit: (*top*) side view, between eye and nostril; (*middle*) head-on view; (*bottom*) close-up. Diagram (*right*) is cross-section of pit's structure.

The American copperhead is inoffensive and of retiring disposition, but if provoked may bite savagely. This snake is feared because of its fast strike; the bite is rarely fatal, although it produces much discoloration of the tissues and long-lasting symptoms. When furious, the copperhead vibrates its tail and in among dead leaves and twigs can sound much like a rattlesnake.

The American copperhead emerges from hibernation in April. The mating season follows soon after, a small number of young, usually about five, being born in August. In the autumn, large numbers of copperheads may collect in a single den to hibernate and commonly keep company with timber rattlesnakes.

The Cottonmouth *(Agkistrodon piscivorus),* or water moccasin, is found in the southeastern United States, mainly in the swamplands of Mississippi and in Florida. It grows just over three feet long on average, but one or two are on record nearly six feet long. The cottonmouth is scarcely ever found away from the vicinity of water but may be seen basking on banks or logs protruding from the water in swamps or slow-moving waters. As might be expected from

American Copperhead

Cottonmouth, or Water Moccasin

its habitat, the cottonmouth eats frogs, fish, and baby terra-pins and any other small backboned animals that can be caught near water.

The bite of the cottonmouth can be lethal; as it is sluggish and rarely moves away if disturbed, it is a dangerous snake. Luckily, when molested, it normally goes through a threat-display before actually biting. This display consists of gap-ing widely, showing the inside of its mouth, which is white and contrasts vividly with the body color. It is this that gives this snake its name.

The cottonmouth mates in March and produces about eight young at the beginning of September. These are about seven inches long and early in life are brightly banded with a yellow tail that probably functions as a lure.

The Fer-de-lance (*Bothrops atrox*) is found from southern Mexico southward to Peru. This deadly snake grows to a maximum length of over eight feet, but many adult speci-mens do not exceed four feet. The usual food is rats and sometimes these are hunted near human habitation, al-though normally the fer-de-lance lives in forest areas. In those parts of South America where there is cultivation, this snake has invaded sugar plantations, presumably feeding on the rats that infest the crop.

Fer-de-lance

The fer-de-lance gives birth to 50 or more young at a time, each fully capable of giving a venomous bite within minutes of being born. The venom of the fer-de-lance is particularly powerful and fast-acting; because of it, this snake is very much feared. Nowadays, treatment is usually possible if the victim is found soon enough, but the fatality rate used to be high. There are many snakes in tropical America belonging to the same genus.

The Bushmaster (*Lachesis muta*) inhabits tropical South America and the southern parts of Central America. It is the largest species of viper in the world; the biggest specimens grow over 12 feet long, although eight or nine feet is a more usual length. The bushmaster is, however, proportionately much slimmer than many of the vipers and an adult may weigh little more than a large rattlesnake or Gaboon viper. It is unusual among the viperids — and unique among the

New World viperids—in that it lays eggs rather than giving birth to living young. A female bushmaster lays approximately 12 eggs and usually remains in the vicinity of the nest, possibly acting as a guard.

The bite of a bushmaster can be very dangerous, producing death in a few hours, but they are not common snakes and are unlikely to be encountered. They may move toward anything they are intent on biting; because of their large size, they can also strike from a great distance. The scientific name of this snake means 'silent fate,' a suitably sinister name for a potentially dangerous reptile. Actually, the bushmaster may not always be silent, as although it lacks the elaborate sound-producing device of the rattlesnakes, it has a pointed hard tail which it vibrates at great speed. Among leaves or similar debris, a high-pitched buzz may be produced.

Small mammals make up the bulk of the food of the bushmaster and these are captured by ambush along their trails. The bushmaster is mainly a creature of the forests and woods but is occasionally found outside wooded areas.

The Jumping Viper *(Bothrops nummifer),* or tommygoff, lives in Central America and Mexico. It has a short, thickset body that seldom exceeds three feet and is covered with very rough scales.

This viper receives its name from its ability to hurl itself

Bushmaster

at an assailant. The jumping viper is quick-tempered; if disturbed, it first coils, then springs by suddenly straightening its body, aiming a bite at its adversary. By this means, it may actually leave the ground for a short distance although it usually drags its tail as it lurches forward. By 'jumping' in this way, the viper can propel itself two or three feet forward.

In spite of these vicious attacks, the snake is comparatively harmless, as its venom is not strong and the fangs are short. Still, it is not a serpent to treat lightly, even though the natives in some parts of its range say that it is harmless.

The genus *Trimeresurus* includes some 25 species found in southeast Asia from China through India to Ceylon. This genus is closely related to the New World genus *Bothrops* (with its thirty or more species) and at one time the two groups were both classified together. All the species of *Trimeresurus* are small and not especially stout snakes, growing to about three feet long. Many are terrestrial with a tendency toward drab gray and brown coloration. But some are arboreal and these are usually equipped with a highly prehensile tail and a green coloration, presumably camouflage for hiding among leaves.

Jumping Viper

The Temple Viper *(Trimeresurus wagleri),* or Wagler's pit-viper, is found from the Malay Peninsula to the Philippines and on most of the East Indian islands with the exception of Java. It grows to three feet long. The temple viper is common in low-lying jungles and spends much of its time climbing in low bushes. It is generally a sluggish animal, but can climb well using its prehensile tail; it captures small birds, mammals, and arboreal lizards to eat.

The temple viper acquires its name from its occurrence in the Snake Temple on the island of Penang. In this temple, the snakes are not molested and are allowed to remain climbing around and in the temple, where they may be seen sometimes in large numbers. In spite of their number and their proximity to worshipers in the temple, the snakes never seem to bite. The same species of snake is considered to bring good luck in parts of Borneo and Sumatra and sometimes they are kept by the natives in trees close to their homes. The temple viper

Temple vipers in a Malayan temple.

seems remarkably good-tempered and rarely bites unless it is handled very roughly. The venom is, in any case, seldom fatal but the bite can still be excruciatingly painful and a large amount of swelling may take place, especially near the bite.

Rattlesnakes

The rattlesnakes belong to the genus *Crotalus* and are a mainly North American group of snakes consisting of about 20 species, most of which can be found within the borders of the United States. Rattlesnakes are found mostly in the drier parts of the southern and western United States, but two species are found in the east and some rattlers also penetrate to tropical South America. Rattlesnakes belong to the pit-viper division of the viper family; all have a heat-sensitive pit in their face. The characteristic that marks off the rattlesnakes from all other snakes, though, is the peculiar development of the tail to form a rattle. Rattlesnakes, like other snakes, are deaf and they cannot hear their own rattle or that of other snakes, so they cannot communicate by rattling. The rattle seems to be used by the rattlesnake for warning away other animals for, suddenly confronted with the strange sound of an angry rattler vibrating its tail, an animal may hesitate to attack or, being warned of the presence of the snake, can avoid treading on it.

The rattle is made by specialized scales at the end of the tail. A baby rattler is born with a hard button-like scale at the tip of the tail; this is shed at the first sloughing and replaced, the young rattler being still without a rattle. At the next shedding of the skin, the button is not lost but remains attached to the new hard scale formed over the tip of the tail. When the snake sloughs its skin again, the end-scale of the tail remains attached to the new tail tip. This process continues at each subsequent molt until the rattlesnake has a tail appendage made up of several segments; each interlocks with the next but each is dead, dry, and hollow and capable of being rattled against its neighbor to produce the characteristic rattlesnake sound. The sound produced by a rattlesnake is not so much a rattle as a buzz or whirring noise. When the snake is really angry, the tail is wagged so fast it becomes just a blur.

A rattlesnake sheds its skin three or four times a year during the early years of its life; as it adds a new segment to the rattle at each molt, this means that the number of rattles does not relate directly to the age of the snake. Moreover, the end segments usually break off the rattle when it gets to six or seven segments long, and it is unusual to find a snake with as many as a dozen segments.

The rattle of the rattlesnake is produced by the tail segments that interlock one with the other. They are dead and hollow and can be moved against each other to produce the characteristic noise.

There are many snakes that wave their tails when excited—
such as king snakes and the bushmaster among the rattlesnakes' close relations—but only in the rattlesnakes do we
find this special development of the tail for rattling.

The Eastern Diamond Rattlesnake (*Crotalus adamanteus*)
grows to an average length of five feet. The largest specimen
ever measured was nearly nine feet long and ranks as the
largest poisonous snake in North America. In these large
rattlesnakes, like the big vipers, the fangs may be anything
up to an inch long. The eastern diamond rattlesnake is
found in the southeastern United States, south from the
Carolinas and west to Louisiana. It is never found more than
100 miles from the coast. Its habitat is mainly brush country
where there is little disturbance from man; although it
does not like swampy land, it will nevertheless live adjacent
to it. It is a rather sluggish snake but it can be dangerous,

especially because it may not rattle until it is very closely approached and does not move away from trouble but always stands its ground. If necessary, this snake will defend itself very ferociously.

The eastern diamond rattlesnake feeds mainly on rabbits but it will occasionally include other small mammals and birds in its diet. About ten young, each just over a foot long, are born at a time.

The Western Diamond Rattlesnake *(Crotalus atrox)* is a little smaller than its eastern counterpart, never exceeding seven feet in length and averaging only about four feet six inches. It lives in deserts and prairies from Mississippi to California, and is found around the edges of mountain ranges but never at any great height. It is an aggressive snake, quick to take alarm, rattle, and coil, and ready to strike when it is within range. As it is widely spread and relatively common,

Western Diamond Rattlesnake

the aggressive temperament of this snake causes it to be one of the most frequent causes of snakebite and the main contribution to snake venom deaths in North America.

Normally, though, it saves its poison to acquire its food, mainly rabbits but also some rodents and birds.

The Sidewinder *(Crotalus cerastes)* is found in the deserts of the southwest United States where it lives on the loose shifting sands. It is sometimes known as the horned rattlesnake because of the horn above each eye that may help to shade the eye and stop sand drifting over it as the snake lies almost buried. The sidewinder is usually about a foot and a half long but may grow a foot longer than this. Unusually for this group of snakes, the largest specimens are females.

Because it is a nocturnal snake and lies buried in the heat of the day, the sidewinder is rarely seen. However, quite often in the mornings, the sand hills are crossed by the J-shaped tracks that mark the progress of the snake the previous night.

The Timber Rattlesnake *(Crotalus horridus),* or banded rattlesnake, is found in the eastern United States and was the first 'rattler' encountered by the early colonists of North America, who sent back rather exaggerated stories of its

Sidewinder Rattlesnake

size and attributes. It is not a very large snake, usually growing no more than forty inches long. It has a rather irregular distribution, partly because it has been pushed out from some of its haunts by human interference, and partly because its chosen habitat is rocky limestone country covered with timber. In spite of this, it remains the commonest of all the rattlesnakes in the United States.

Although it may bite if cornered, the timber rattlesnake is generally of peaceable disposition. It feeds mostly on mice but adds variety to its diet by eating squirrels and rabbits. In the winter many timber rattlesnakes may congregate in a single den to hibernate, and numbers running into hundreds have been seen in one place.

The Prairie Rattlesnake *(Crotalus viridis)* lives in the western parts of the United States and southwestern Canada. This species is aptly named as it makes its home in the prairies, moving, for a snake, considerable distances in search of the rodents that form its food. The prairie rattlesnake varies in length in different parts of its range but is never more than five feet long. It is generally not afraid to show itself,

Timber Rattlesnake

Prairie Rattlesnake

and as it moves about in the daytime it is quite often seen. When winter comes, these snakes retreat below the ground, often using marmot or prairie dog burrows in which to hibernate.

Like other rattlesnakes, the prairie rattlesnake is ovoviviparous, giving birth to an average of twelve young at a time. An interesting characteristic is that in the northern part of its range development of the young is so slow that they are carried inside the mother for a year longer than in the south, where development takes a matter of months.

The Pigmy Rattlesnake (*Sistrurus miliarius*) is found in the southeastern United States. It is only 18 inches long—or two and a half feet at the most—and it is in some ways less specialized and different from the other rattlesnakes. Instead of having its head covered with small scales like most rattlers and vipers, the pigmy rattlesnake has head-shields like a harmless colubrid. The rattle is also not so well developed and is proportionately smaller; the noise it makes, a high-pitched buzz, is audible only at a short distance from the snake. The venom glands are small and the bite is not fatal, although cases have been known of a pigmy rattlesnake bite giving rise to unpleasant symptoms whose effects lasted for months. Although the snake is small, it is very quick-tempered.

The pigmy rattlesnake eats small lizards and snakes, rarely troubling to use its venom on these. It also eats mice and these are usually stabbed by the fangs.

This snake gives birth to about nine young at a time. The baby snakes are only just over five inches in length, but grow quite rapidly.

A relative, **the Massasauga Rattler** *(Sistrurus catenatus),* is slightly larger but less aggressive than the pigmy rattlesnake. Its range is in the Midwest, from the Great Lakes down through Texas.

Pigmy Rattlesnake

145

SNAKES AND MAN

Along with their many other distinctive attributes, snakes are remarkable for the strength of emotion they have always aroused in people. Some people are fond of snakes, but such individuals form a minority. Most people regard snakes with mild distaste, and a surprisingly large proportion of people loathe them. A recent survey in Great Britain showed that more than a quarter of children disliked snakes more than any other animal; the proportion of adults is probably nearly as high. Yet in Britain, as in the United States, there is little danger of snake-bite and most of the reasons given by people for disliking snakes are highly irrational. For example, people claim that they are slimy or dirty when of course they are neither. This dislike of snakes seems to be something that is learned from other people and not acquired from contact with snakes themselves.

In various parts of the world, men make a living by cashing in on man's awe of snakes. The snake-charmer

Young children have little instinctive fear of snakes, but even a chimpanzee reared in a zoo will try to avoid a snake if confronted with it.

The flute of the Indian snake-charmer cannot be heard by the snake, which responds to the man's movement.

relies on the fact that people are prepared to pay to watch him handle animals that they themselves fear. Sometimes the snakes exhibited by a charmer are harmless species, but often they are potentially poisonous. Some of the less reputable charmers work with specimens that have had their fangs removed or even the front of the jaws terribly mutilated. But many charmers work with intact snakes and need quite a bit of skill to carry out their work. Some snake-charmers may build up a little resistance to venom by allowing themselves to receive many small doses, but with all of these charmers there still remains the possibility of a bite ending in death.

In spite of the dislike of snakes found in modern times in many lands, snakes have in various times and places been welcomed or even venerated as gods. In Africa, India, South America, and Europe, snakes have been worshiped. Some of the ancient Greek gods were originally snake deities. Man tends to look with awe at anything unusual; the snakes, with their unblinking gaze, locomotion without legs, and ability in some cases to kill with a single bite, are sufficiently odd and unlike man to inspire respect. Furthermore, snakes shed their skins and this has given rise to the belief that they can be 'born again.' For this reason, snakes have become symbols of health and life, and many snake cults associate them with fertility. A frequent belief—arising as far apart as ancient Egypt and the Australian aborigines—supposes snakes or snake gods to be the bringers of rain or water to the land. The cobra—goddess Ejo—was worshiped by the Egyptians and featured in the headdress of the ruler. In most cases, the snakes were powers for good, although their evil side might show up by withholding their beneficial influence.

Snakes are associated with fertility and are an important part of many native cults—as here, in the snake dance of the Hopi Indians of the American Southwest.

Even today, the Hopi Indians of Arizona perform a snake dance originally designed to bring rain. Snakes, including rattlesnakes, are held in the mouth by the priests as they dance at the end of nine days' ritual.

Even where snakes have not been worshiped, they have been widely used as symbols, good luck charms, or as magical

The snake-entwined caduceus was the symbol of Mercury and a snake is also featured in Egyptian headdresses.

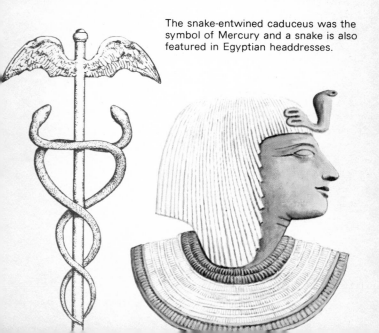

medicine. In medieval times, practically every organ of a snake was considered good for one ailment or another; even today, some people believe snake oil or fat, used as a liniment, will produce healing suppleness.

The Greek god of healing and medicine, Aesculapius, had a snake twined around a staff as his symbol; today this same symbol is still in use as the symbol of the medical profession. The caduceus, symbol of the messenger god Mercury, was two snakes entwined around a staff, and was a sign of peace.

In reputable medicine today, of course, snakes have little use. Some venoms have been tested for use as drugs, but mostly they are too variable and impure to be much good. Russell's viper venom has been used as a blood coagulant to stop severe bleeding.

It is estimated that every year, throughout the whole world, 30,000 people die of snake-bite. This sounds a large number but is only a tiny fraction of the world population; for that matter, it is only a small percentage of the number of people bitten by poisonous snakes every year. Death by snake-bite is extremely unlikely, even in Burma, the country with the highest death rate from this cause, infested with snakes and with a largely barefoot population.

Nevertheless, much suffering is caused from snake-bites each year. The cobra family are probably the most dangerous to humans, but the venom of the viper family has more unpleasant symptoms. All venoms are a mixture of many substances, but in the venom of cobras and seasnakes neurotoxins predominate. These are nerve poisons and may cause a feeling of weakness and a paralysis that may extend to the muscles used in breathing and those of the heart, causing death mainly by suffocation. There is little pain, and consciousness is usually retained to the end. In cobra venom, there are also substances that break down red corpuscles in the blood and work to stop the blood coagulating.

In viper venom, hemotoxins predominate. These are substances that attack blood corpuscles and break down the cells of the blood vessel linings and substances that cause the blood to clot internally. The symptoms are painful, involving burning sensations at the bite, swelling that may double the size of a limb, and discoloration of the tissues where they are attacked by venom to blues, reds, or even black and green. The main danger comes from internal bleeding or from weakening of the heart, which usually develops a fast but feeble pulse.

Recovery from cobra bite is normally complete, but viper bite can, because of the tissue damage it causes, leave long-lasting or even permanent effects. Probably in most cases the worst effect of a snake-bite is a state of shock and fear in the recipient; people have been known to die, apparently from shock, after a bite from a harmless snake.

Many remedies for snake-bite have been advocated over the last few hundred years. In most cases, the remedy has been worse than the bite—for example, amputation of the bitten limb, or administration of large amounts of alcohol, liable to cause a fast pulse or even alcohol poisoning. Even apparently sensible precautions like sucking the bite or administering potassium permanganate, which neutralizes venom in a test tube, are actually of little value; the venom is so rapidly absorbed from the bite into the bloodstream that only a very little remains at the site to be tackled.

In cases of snake-bite, the offending reptile should be killed and kept for identification, being handled only by the tail. Medical aid should be summoned immediately; in the meantime, the patient should be kept in a state of complete rest, with a bitten limb hanging down and kept still to minimize blood flow. It is helpful to apply a tourniquet around a limb above the bite, but this should only be tight enough to impede blood flow in the veins and not the arteries; the tourniquet should be released every few minutes. The object of all the first aid for bites of this kind is to slow down the spread of poison, if possible, until a doctor arrives with an antidote.

Nowadays, antidotes to the venom of many of the world's poisonous snakes are available. These are produced by inoculating an experimental animal, nearly always a horse, with small doses of venom. Gradually the animal builds up a resistance in its blood to the venom. Eventually it can withstand, with no ill-effects, an injection of venom that would be lethal to an untreated animal, as its blood can attack the

Snake farms keep many snakes for their venom in small, cool, domed houses.

venom and render it harmless. Blood serum transferred from immunized horses can be injected into bitten humans and again will go about the business of neutralizing venom. This antivenom serum is known as antivenin.

Antivenin is usually very effective against snake-bite if used quickly enough. Its main disadvantage is that a small proportion of people are allergic to horse serum; in these people, antivenin may have worse effects than the bite. (The only person to die following a snake-bite in Great Britain since World War II died from the effects of serum, not the bite.) If care is taken with its administration, antivenin should normally provide a complete cure.

In several places in the world there are now institutes devoted to the production of antivenin and to further research into venoms. One of the main troubles is that every snake species has its own characteristic venom; differences between venoms are so great that it is impossible to produce a single antivenin to act against all kinds of bite. For a single area of the world, though, it is usually possible to provide a polyvalent antivenin, which can be used against, say, most of the vipers liable to be encountered.

To make antivenin, it is necessary to have large supplies of venom and therefore regular supplies of poisonous snakes. To a certain extent demand is satisfied by offering rewards for live poisonous snakes, but most institutes researching into venom also maintain their own snake 'farms.' Large numbers of snakes are kept in escape-proof compounds in which are small domed houses where they tend to congregate in the dark. When snakes are required for venom, the domes are lifted and the snakes inside are taken to have their venom extracted by the process known as 'milking.'

This simple, but skilled, operation is carried out by seizing the snake correctly behind the head and then opening its mouth or inducing it to bite through a membrane into a small cup. While the fangs are in the cup, the head of the snake is pressed gently to force venom from the glands down the fangs. The snake is then taken away and allowed plenty of time to manufacture new venom before being used again.

Most of the research into venom is concerned with the numerous species of snake found in the tropics, but antivenin is also made for use against the snakes found in more populated regions such as North America and Europe.

'Milking' a snake for its venom is a simple but skilled operation.

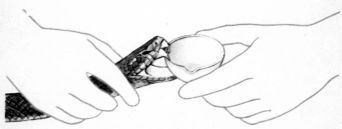

Although snakes may often be a nuisance to humans if they are poisonous or if they kill poultry, they also have a useful side. Perhaps their chief economic importance is in the destruction of rodents. Rat snakes are welcomed by North American farmers for this reason; pythons are no less welcome in some parts of Asia, where they may be deliberately placed in grain stores to discourage rats.

From time immemorial, too, the skins of snakes have been used as leather. Snakes are fairly simple to skin, although this should be done as soon as possible after death. It is only necessary to slit the snake down the middle of the belly and pull off the skin. Snake skin does not retain its bright colors after death, but the beautiful patterning to be seen on many species remains.

Snakes are also extensively used as food. In the Western world, where there is no general shortage of meat, we tend to underuse our natural animal resources and frown on unusual meats. In less devel-

The most popular snakes for leather are the pythons.

154

oped parts of the world people have neither acquired, nor can afford, our peculiar prejudices and do not so readily pass over a chance of easily killed meat. The large constricting snakes are the most frequent source of food—anacondas and boa constrictors in South America, and large pythons in Africa, Asia, and Australia; in the Far East, such fare as kraits, king cobras, and other cobras are eaten and enjoyed. Certain snakes are considered special delicacies when they are in good fat condition in the autumn. There is plenty of meat and also much fat on the larger snakes, and it is possible to make a good meal from them.

Among the developed countries, only the United States makes much use of snakes as food, but there is only a limited small-scale demand for rattlesnake meat. It is possible to buy cans of rattlesnake meat if desired. Apparently good food, 'rattler steaks' were eaten by early settlers, but nowadays they are pretty much restricted to novelties at cocktail parties and similar gatherings.

Snake leather can be made into a variety of goods.

BOOKS TO READ

There are numerous books on snakes, from highly technical works for specialists to introductions for young people. We can offer only a sampling of the more accessible ones—in terms of availability, price, and level of difficulty—to the North American reader.

The Reptiles. Archie Carr. Time-Life Books, 1963.
Poisonous Snakes of the World. Department of the Navy. Goverment Printing Office.
The Reptile World. Clifford H. Pope. Knopf, 1956.
Living Reptiles of the World. Karl Schmidt and Robert Inger. Doubleday, 1957.
Amphibians and Reptiles of Western North America. Robert C. Stebbins. McGraw-Hill, 1954.
Reptiles and Amphibians: A Guide to Familiar Species. Herbert Zim and Hobart Smith. Golden Press, 1953.

PLACES TO VISIT

There is no denying that certain snakes are dangerous enough to discourage most people from tracking down any snakes in their natural habitats. Fortunately, we can view snakes safely in zoos and museums; we offer here a list of largest collections in North America.

Zoos
California: San Diego Zoological Park. *Florida:* Miami, The Serpentarium. Silver Springs, Ross Allen's Reptile Institute. *Illinois:* Chicago, The Brookfield Zoo; Lincoln Park Zoo. *New York:* New York City, The Bronx Zoo; Staten Island Zoo. *Pennsylvania:* Philadelphia Zoological Park. *Texas:* San Antonio Zoo. *Washington, D. C.:* National Zoological Park.

Museums
California: Berkeley, University of California Museum of Vertebrate Zoology; Los Angeles County Museum. *Illinois:* Chicago, Natural History Museum. *Massachusetts:* Cambridge, Harvard Museum of Comparative Zoology. *Michigan:* Ann Arbor, University of Michigan Museum of Zoology. *New York:* New York City, The American Museum of Natural History. *Washington, D. C.:* The National Museum.

INDEX